The Marketing

THE MARKETING LEADER'S CODE

Unlock your potential - Learn the secrets of successful marketing leadership

GARETH HELM

Sideminds.com

First published in 2023 by Intellectual Perspective Press (www.intellectualperspective.com).

Illustrations by Sophie Helm.

CONTENTS

Author's Note vii

The Marketing Leader's CODE Reviews viii

Introduction: Don't lose your job x

PART 1: Decoding the Marketing Leader's role

Welcome to the toughest job 3

Navigating the marketing leadership role 9

Taking the assessment 15

PART 2: Discover what the Marketing Leader's CODE means

ANCHOR Factors 25

Ambition ANCHOR Factor 28

Network ANCHOR Factor 35

Capability ANCHOR Factor 43

Headspace ANCHOR Factor 51

Output ANCHOR Factor 59

Results ANCHOR Factor 65

The Marketing Leader's CODE 71

Connector led marketing leaders 73

Operator led marketing leaders 76
Disruptor led marketing leaders 79
Explorer led marketing leaders 82

PART 3: Using the Marketing Leader's CODE

Interpreting your results 87
Understanding your CODE 87
Enhancing your Leadership Team impact 90
Onboarding or recruiting a new marketing leader 94
Becoming a future marketing leader 97
Tactics to try 100
Connector Tactics 101
Operator Tactics 105
Disruptor Tactics 109
Explorer Tactics 113
Next steps and further support 117
About the author 119
References 120
Appendix 125
Acknowledgements 133

AUTHOR'S NOTE

Do you want the top job in marketing and be successful long term?

Are you a business leader wanting to get the most out of marketing?

Are you an ambitious marketer wanting to be a future marketing leader?

Are you a recruiter looking to improve your marketing leader recruitment success rates?

The Marketing Leader's CODE is a leadership book for marketing leaders, written by marketing leaders. Much has been published about the challenges marketing leaders face, but very little has been done to prepare marketers for the leadership role and be successful. This book fills this gap by distilling the activities of successful marketing leaders into a simple framework and providing diagnostic assessments, real-life case studies and a toolkit of tactics to build capability.

Further detailed assessments and support are available at www.sideminds.com or www.linkedin.com/company/sideminds.

THE MARKETING LEADER'S CODE REVIEWS

'I am a big believer in marketing being the engine of business growth and CMOs being the key. Gareth is the absolute role model in delivering this and his approach is revealed in The Marketing Leader's CODE. This excellent book is a must read for every marketing person.' Richard Harpin, Founder and CEO, HomeServe PLC.

'This book makes being an effective marketing leader a whole lot easier.' Richard Reed, Co-founder Innocent Drinks and Jam Jar Investments.

'A very insightful guide for senior marketing leaders on how to think about the best way to interact with and deliver results to the wider organisation.' Alex Chesterman OBE, Founder and CEO Cazoo and formerly Zoopla.

'Gareth's unique toolkit will prove hugely valuable for every CMO who seeks more impact'. Thomas Barta, Co-author The 12 Powers of a Marketing Leader.

'An essential read for marketing leaders packed full of great practical tools and tips that you can start using to drive real and immediate impact.' Peter Markey, CMO Boots

'There are many leadership books but not many focus on unique challenges CMOs face. This book fills this gap and provides a very helpful framework to navigate one of the most transient roles in the C-suite.' Yilmaz Erceyes, CMO Premier Foods

'An amazing tool for new marketers to help them understand this new marketing world... ..it would have helped me identify and anticipate some political issues, manage egos, and simply plan better.' Antoinette Benoit, Former CMO McDonald's

'A hugely compelling and valuable career support for marketing leaders.' Colin Whaley, Sales and Marketing Director, Center Parcs

'The Marketing Leader's CODE helps future marketing leaders understand what is necessary to make an impact at board level.' Ben Caunter, Senior Vice President & Head of International Marketing, IMAX Corporation

'A very practical and helpful resource for anyone who is or wants to be a senior marketing leader.' Richard Coles, Digital Director, Greene King & Former CMO, Caxton

'The honesty together with the really actionable advice, make the book an essential read for all CMOs.' Joanne Savage, Director Marketing EMEA, Fitbit at Google

'We live in an age of ambiguity – in marketing, business and in life. Gareth Helm goes beyond the usual vaugeries to tackle the nuts and bolts of marketing skills with cool precision. The result is less a book than a crash course. It will help you to self-diagnose quickly and build a regimen of improvement to make you smarter and stronger. It's invaluable!' Colin Mitchell, CIO VMG and formerly SVP, Global Marketing, McDonald's

'This book is vital navigation. It's a practical guide to effective co-steering and reinforces the need for empathy and a shared perspective at every level. If only I'd had it sooner!' Philippa Heywood, Managing Director, Thortful

'As a fast growth business our marketing needs continue to evolve and change. The Marketing Leader's CODE has helped me think through what we need from our marketing leadership at each stage as we level up.' Jonathan Petrides, Founder and CEO of allplants

INTRODUCTION: DON'T LOSE YOUR JOB

As a fledgling marketer starting out, I always dreamed of one day getting a company's top job in marketing, coming up with the strategy, making the decisions, spending the budget. Eventually I managed it. I became the marketing leader at Innocent Drinks, then Mars, and Zoopla. I was moving up in the marketing world. Then I became the Chief Marketing Officer for McDonald's in the UK and Ireland, and as I sat behind my desk after a strong set of business results and a positive year-end review, I could finally say 'I'm lovin' it'.

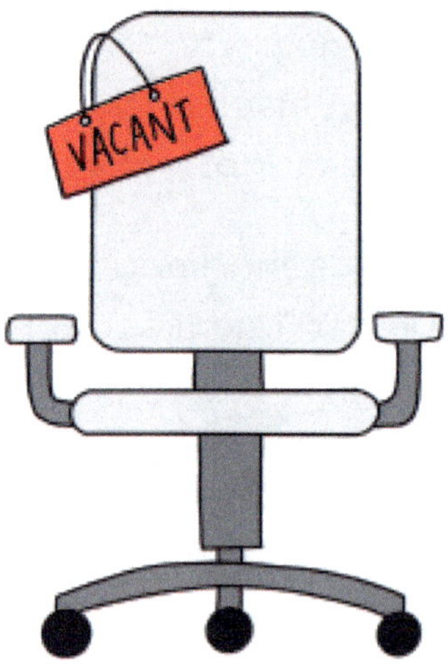

A few months later and my job was gone. This *top job* was not quite what I had thought. What a shock. What had made me effective and successful in one leadership position and less so now?

On a simplistic level I could explain my job loss by pointing to the re-organisation of the global and local marketing function, which lead to the UK and Ireland Chief Marketing Officer position being removed. It was a plausible narrative that explained my relatively short tenure, but I knew at a more objective level there was far more going on. I may have ticked the boxes of a year-end review, but as I reflected, I had not built enough of a connection with the UK CEO and Leadership Team. My value was not percolating through and I was vulnerable. It was frustrating and as I approached a new job, now as a Global Chief Marketing Officer, I did not want this to happen again so I started to consolidate what I had learnt about being the marketing leader. **What was really going on and what were the lessons for every marketer as they aspire to this leadership position?**

I reflected on my experiences, read around the subject and talked to my marketing peers. There turned out to be a large collection of published material explaining the challenges marketing leaders face. Kimberly Whitler's *The Trouble With CMOs*[1] summarised an underlying issue:

'Something is going very wrong in the relationship between CEOs and CMOs... ...80% of CEOs don't trust or are unimpressed by their CMO. In comparison, just 10% of the same CEOs feel the same way about their CFOs and CIOs.'

The Marketing Society[2] recognise this and call it out in the first section of their first 100 days (F100D) guide '*why are the first 100 days so hard for marketers'.* Spencer Stuart annually publishes a report on the tenure of CMOs[3] which shows **the median tenure for top marketers is now just over 2 years**, the lowest of the entire Leadership Team. You do not see anything like this for finance, sales people or operational leaders.

Many of my peer base seemed to have experienced something similar and my short tenure at McDonald's was in fact normal. Marketing leadership jobs are very volatile, and no psychometric pre-assessment or interview can really assess how you will fit in with the Leadership Team.

What a terrible waste of time and effort for everyone involved if marketing leaders churn within a couple of years and aren't trusted by their CEO. This isn't good for anyone. It doesn't need to and shouldn't be like this.

Losing my job was part of a wider spread problem, but where are the guidebooks and advice services to support marketers in this challenging position? Most senior marketers dust themselves down and go again at a new role. I was the same, but as I prepared, I decided to pick apart my experiences and the experiences of my peers and wider industry experts to create a framework for success. Two years later and *The Marketing Leader's CODE* has been created. This explains the challenges the marketing leader faces, provides a capability structure to the marketing leadership role and gives guidance on how problems can be overcome. This framework is based on a combination of practical first-hand experience with references to broader publications on marketing and leadership where relevant.

The Marketing Leader's CODE organises success factors into a CODE made up of 4 essential genres: Connector, Operator, Disruptor and Explorer. Each genre is further divided into 3 ANCHOR Factors, where ANCHOR is an acronym for pairs of essential marketing leadership capabilities and behaviours the marketer needs to deliver. ANCHOR Factors have over the last 2 years been tested and validated with a large marketing peer set.

Every marketing role and every Leadership Team is different, so the blend of ANCHOR Factors needed is different, which changes the CODE and ultimately success in the role. This individual blend can be determined through the assessments in this book and online.

The CODE also starts to demystify the differences between the Chief Marketing Officer, Chief Digital Officer, Chief Growth Officer, Chief Customer Officer, Chief Brand Officer and Chief Strategy Officer. Each of these roles have different weights of ANCHOR Factors and knowing this can help the CEO or Leadership Team decide what type of marketer they really need.

The Marketing Leader's CODE is presented on a circular map. The map can be used to help existing marketing leaders build their capability, enhance onboarding a new leader, improve recruitment and internal dialogue about the marketing function and enable future marketing leaders build their career to the Leadership Team by using tactics and tools highlighted later in the book. A tool to help the marketing leader be more effective and successful over the long term.

The Marketing Leader's CODE

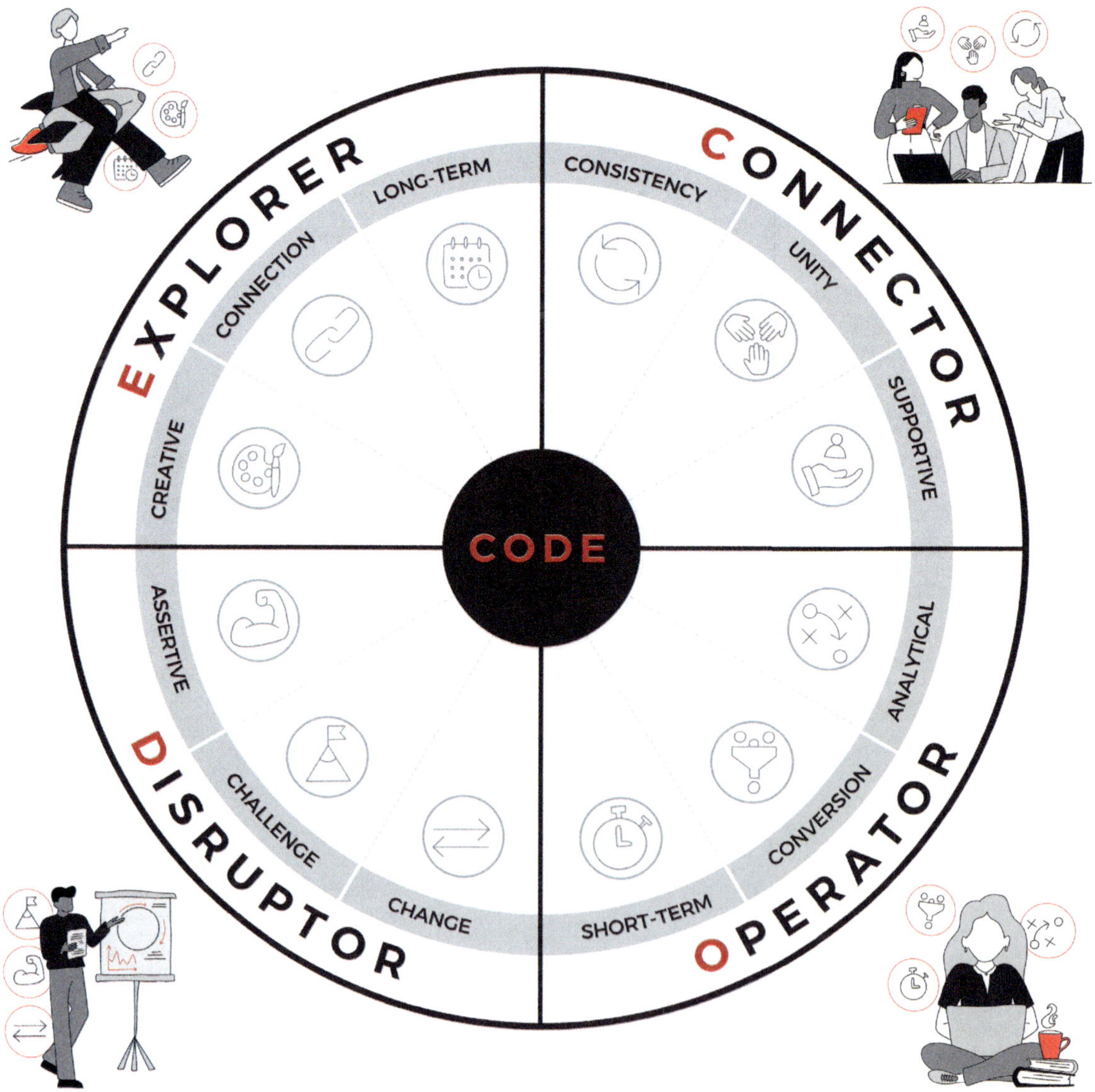

Notes

1. Whitler, K., and Morgan, N. (July- August, 2017). *The trouble with CMOs*. Harvard Business Review. https://hbr.org/2017/07/the-trouble-with-cmos
2. Market Leader (Spring 2006). *Empower*. The Marketing Society. http://www.marketingsociety.com/the-library/marketing-directors-first-100-days/
3. Welch, G., and Sanderson, R. (April, 2022). *CMO Tenure Study: Women outnumber men for first time in CMO role*. Spencer Stuart. https://www.spencerstuart.com/research-and-insight/cmo-tenure-study-women-outnumber-men-for-first-time-in-cmo-role

PART 1: DECODING THE MARKETING LEADER'S ROLE

WELCOME TO THE TOUGHEST JOB

So, you're the Top Dog in marketing. Congratulations, you got the job!

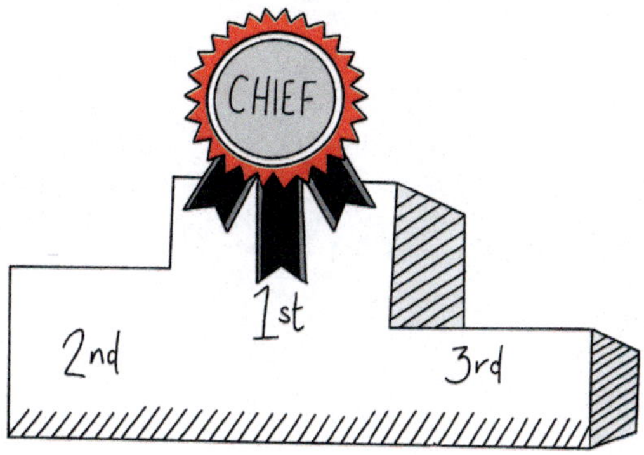

Now for the tough bit. You need to realise the role is often misunderstood and sometimes undervalued by many of your colleagues in the Leadership Team. No other leadership role has experienced so much change in the last 10 years:

- marketing channels and customer journeys have expanded into areas some of the Leadership Team have not heard about and will not understand,
- the speed of change is accelerating, so innovation must accelerate too, with marketing either spearheading or being integral into cross functional agile teams,
- there is more business and customer data than ever before, giving the marketer richer insight but less time to make critical decisions and get Leadership Team alignment.

PHD Worldwide assessed the capabilities in the role in 2011 vs 2021, which highlighted a change of 51%.[1] That is a lot of change for a marketer, but to a CEO or CFO who has been in business for years this evolution can feel like revolution.

CEOs, after all, mainly come from an operations or finance background and can spend very little time thinking about marketing or appreciate the changes that have taken place. They have been successful in their own right, will have a view on what works and have experienced. Why should they change their business views? Smart, successful people are often the hardest to influence and become defensive and challenging, as shown by Chris Arygris's in the Harvard Business Review[2]:

'Put simply, because many professionals are almost always successful at what they do, they rarely experience failure. And because they have rarely failed, they have never learned how to learn from failure.'

This can make the marketing leader's role a lonely place. Unlike your leadership peers, your success is far less about your functional capability but your ability to lead, shape others' opinions, get collective buy-in and inspire the wider decision makers on a growth agenda. You have two audiences to win over: your external customer audience and your internal leadership audience. Both have their own 'language' and you need to plough energy into being multilingual. Exceptional marketing leaders are more than just great marketers, they are the ultimate bridge between the organisation and the customer, who provide ongoing counsel and guidance to others, constantly ensuring through the ups and downs of a business calendar that the decision makers are informed and aligned across all departments and channels.

This highlights an important marketing leader truth: exceptional marketing has got you into this top position, now it is exceptional leadership that will keep you there.

But you already knew that. Still want the job? Of course you do, so read on and find out what you need to do to be effective in the Leadership Team.

Finding your sea legs

When you join the Leadership Team it is like joining the officers on a boat. The entire crew are under your command, you need to establish yourself and earn their respect and trust of the wider organisation, not just the marketing team. The boat will have a steady rotational motion that you need to get used to and you have to find your sea legs, so you can walk steadily and confidently without feeling disorientated (or seasick!).

Some marketers seem to get it quickly. They find their feet, get quick wins and gain momentum, whilst for others it takes longer, it is more jittery and start-stop. In my last client-side role I worked with a dozen Leadership Teams around the world and it was not always clear which marketers would find their feet and which would not. Two marketers could appear similar on paper but when they joined the Leadership Team things changed. The two adapted differently to the yawing, rolling and pitching of the boat. For the slow starters it can be quite demoralising and lead to a downward cycle.

There is a shift when you become part of the Leadership Team. It is not easy for everyone to do. It can be hard to find your place, but once you do and become part of a unified, motivated and focused team you can make amazing things happen. One inspirational speaker about leadership and diversity is René Carayol MBE. He captures this shift from manager to leader in his book *Spike*[3] and one quote has always resonated:

'Leadership is the art of accomplishing more than the science of management says is possible.'

The speed of business today means the faster you find your feet the better. There will no doubt be a scheduled onboarding plan, but the pace of change does not slow and decisions will need to be made. From day 1 the marketing leader is on display and people are watching how you will behave. You will probably have the expectation of making an impact within 100 days. Why 100 days I have never worked out. I find it shorter in a turn-around business or longer if a complex large scale business, but either way you need to quickly establish yourself within the Leadership Team and find your narrative. In other words find where you are going to focus your effort and then test and validate your thinking.

If this is your first leadership role, you are shifting from being a marketing practitioner to becoming the Leadership Team's influential customer-conscience. This is a profound shift from management of the marketing team to steering the boat with the other officers. A shift where you need to show you have the muscle to push back as well as unify the Leadership Team on not just marketing topics but wider areas too.

If this role is a move between companies and Leadership Teams, you are effectively changing boats and crew, and whilst they may appear familiar to what you have seen before, there will be some very big differences. The awareness and understanding of the marketer's role could be wildly different and the marketer needs to work hard to get accepted. They need to show they empathise with the business, and can keep the immediate day-to-day customer acquisition plan going whilst starting to define future revenue opportunities.

Sound straightforward?

To do this well the marketer needs to draw upon all of their experience and all of their emotional intelligence to read situations and respond in real time. On a boat, like in business, there are tell-tale signs which might seem innocuous but unless dealt with can become issues. Tell-tale comes from the nautical term tell-tail, a piece of string attached to the sailcloth to check the tensions are correct for optimum sailing or in business for optimum performance.

The Marketing Leader's CODE **helps shortcut the process of becoming an established business leader. It decodes the marketing leadership role, so from the outset the boundaries are clear.**

I have lost count of the number of headhunters telling me about exciting companies who are transforming their business with the chief marketer at the heart. The brief often sounds thrilling and is full of marketing buzzwords but frequently the role is ill-defined and unclear. This can be fuelled by a lack of clarity in the Leadership Team, they know they want something different, but it is not clear in the job description and in reality can miss some foundational aspects of the role. This can lead to the wrong marketer joining, which is a disaster for the marketer and the company.

Of course, you would hope good feedback and management would circumnavigate potential issues and help marketers find their feet quickly, but surprisingly with seniority comes less feedback. If there is feedback it can be patchy, indirect or sometimes offloaded inappropriately to a coach to deal with.

I used to get a great deal of indirect feedback at MoneySuperMarket. One exec had a habit of dive bombing me (like a seagull buzzing a chip-eating passenger on a boat) when he had a business concern. He would come circling around to marketing to quiz us. He persistently came back day after day. The same behaviour happened in other teams and you soon realised this was his way of creating focus. Enhancing his awareness of our marketing performance was easy and giving feedback would have been even easier, but sometimes with senior roles this feedback is not voiced.

The Marketing Leader's CODE decodes the role into four essential genres and within each gives key behaviours called ANCHOR Factors. It looks at the marketer's alignment with the business in these key areas and shows real life case studies and tactics to help the marketer be more effective.

Storms will still blow in on the boat, but *The Marketing Leader's CODE* will help the marketer be more prepared, resilient and effective. As Zen Master Thicht Nhat Hanh says:

'In a small boat when a storm comes, if one person remains solid and calm, others will not panic and the boat is more likely to stay afloat.'

Notes

1. PHD Contributors (2022). *Shift. A Marketing Rethink.* PHD Marketing.
2. Argyris, C. (1991). *Teaching smart people how to learn*. Harvard Business Review. https://hbr.org/1991/05/teaching-smart-people-how-to-learn/
3. Carayol, R. (2017). *Spike. What are you great at?* LID Publishing

NAVIGATING THE MARKETING LEADERSHIP ROLE

So how do you decode a role that is increasingly complex and multi-dimensional?

Marketing capability, general management, leadership excellence and a good degree of emotional intelligence all come crashing together in the marketing leadership post. There are no guidebooks on all of this, so I decided to start with my experience and deconstruct the initiatives I had led or been involved in, which had either majorly positive or negative results.

What activities were effective and ineffective in the Leadership Team? What were the sequence of events which led to the subsequent success or failure of an activity? What was the feedback from the Leadership Team or wider business after the activity? What would I do differently next time?

A plethora of projects came to mind. It was a chaotic jumble of good project management, effective collaboration and communication, sound data management and leadership blended with, at the other extreme, creativity, curiosity and a good dash of luck (although good judgement I like to think gives the foundations for luck).

I started to group the information, built various models and stress tested them with my marketing peers, industry experts and published material that was available. Through this iterative process the chaos steadily became organised:

1: Successful marketers require exceptional internal and external communication skills.

In the same way a great marketer can bring 'external' customers around a brand or business initiative, the inverse is also true and the marketing leader needs to break down 'internal' business silos and drive collaboration and alignment around the customer. Internal skills are more about process and influence, sometimes called the 'how', whilst external is about capability and called the 'what'. Both require your energy and drive.

This combination of internal and external capability is called the 'Value Creation Zone' or 'V-Zone' in Thomas Barta and Patrick Barwise's book[1]:

'When marketers work [in the V-Zone], they create value for customers (products, services, and experiences that meet their needs), value for the company (revenue and profit), and value for themselves (greater influence and better careers).'

This led to defining 3 sets of internal and 3 sets of external skills that are essential for the marketing leader.

2: Successful marketers have a skillset of polar opposites.

The marketing leader needs to be inspirational and creative whilst also a sound commercial judge. They need to be challenging and forthright with the Leadership Team, whilst ensuring the Leadership Team have a unified and congruent face for the business. Jim Collins[2] calls this 'Genius of the AND' and what Mark Ritson calls 'Bothism'[3]. As Ritson says:

'If you know anything about marketing you will know that there is an enormous need for Bothism in our discipline right now. We are riven by so many contradictory and combative points of view, most of which would prove more powerful if wrangled into combination rather than opposition.'

This honed the skills into 6 pairs known as ANCHOR Factors, the first 3 are key behaviours and capabilities with their internal business audiences and the last 3 are behaviours and capabilities for the role with their external customer audience. They are called collectively 'ANCHOR Factors', where 'ANCHOR' is a simple acronym for the 6 pairs.

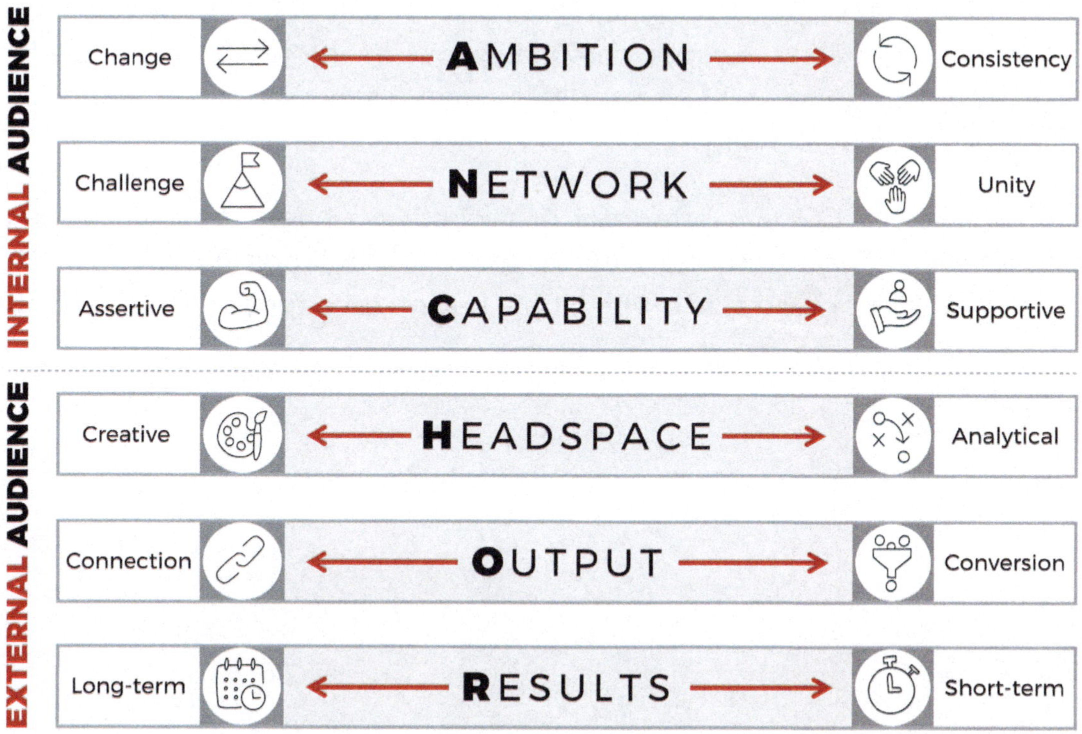

3: Successful marketers often have a skills bias linked to their personality.

Testing the model showed marketers who were strong in one element of an ANCHOR Factor were likely to be strong in other ANCHOR Factors which had the same core underlying traits. For instance the ANCHOR Factors of Change, Challenge and Assertive all had similar underlying traits. So did Consistency, Unity and Supportive, and this continued into Analytical, Conversion and Short-term, and finally Creative, Connection and Long-term.

These behaviours and capabilities if carefully aligned would shoulder onto each other and this created 4 essential genres, Connector, Operator, Disruptor and Explorer or CODE for short.

This is a little like Myers-Briggs, where there are four categories: introversion or extraversion, sensing or intuition, thinking or feeling, judging or perceiving. Everyone has a preference for each category, producing a unique personality type. *The Marketing Leader's CODE* is similar, there are 4 key genres which can differentiate marketers and this has a undying connection to their core personality.

The Marketing Leader's CODE is arranged in a circular wheel. There are four essential genres, Connector, Operator, Disruptor and Explorer and this feeds into 12 ANCHOR Factors, with an ANCHOR Factor on one side of the wheel having an opposite on the other side.

The Marketing Leader's CODE maps the essential capabilities and behaviours to be successful in the marketing leadership role and in the next section the detail behind each area will be explained.

Each marketing leadership job is of course subtly different. The emphasis on each ANCHOR Factor and corresponding CODE will change from role to role, Leadership Team to Leadership Team and CEO to CEO. **To be effective quickly, understanding your CODE and the role's requirements is important, so you are aligned and in sync with those around you.**

To understand your CODE there are two proprietary questionnaires. The first, a mini 12 question assessment, gives you an overview of your CODE. There is also a more detailed version with 60 questions, 5 for each ANCHOR Factor that helps you drill more thoroughly into each part of *The Marketing Leader's CODE,* collect wider 360° feedback and get a recommended development plan. This more detailed version is available online at www.sideminds.com.

Read on to take the mini assessment and find out what this means to you.

Notes

1. Barta, T., and Barwise, P. (2017). *The 12 Powers of a Marketing Leader*. McGraw-Hill Education.
2. Collins, J., and Porras, J. (1995). *Built To Last: Successful Habits of Visionary Companies*. Random House Business.
3. Ritson, M. (September, 2020). *'Bothism' is the cure for marketers' fascination with pointless conflict*. Marketing Week. https://www.marketingweek.com/ritson-bothism-cure-marketers-fascination-conflict/

TAKING THE ASSESSMENT

What type of marketing leader are you and what does the business need? Are you a Connector, who prioritises close relationships with the CEO, Leadership Team and wider business? An Operator, who is into the detail, analysing data and maximising sales? A Disruptor, who is opportunistic and thrives on change or an Explorer, who is strategic, insightful and brand-centric?

Marketing leaders can assess themselves, the marketing leadership role can be assessed or ideally both can be done together using either the mini 'taster' questionnaire printed in this book or the full 60 question version online. The online version is more comprehensive and produces a full report with a recommended development plan.

The marketing leader self-assessment on its own gives a good insight into leadership capabilities across the 12 ANCHOR Factors and CODE genres. **Knowing your CODE and ANCHOR Factors, explains what type of marketing leader you are, so you can find roles that build upon your strengths and allow you to either develop your weaker areas yourself or reset your direct report organisation, so together you are a powerful force.**

This self-assessment can be complemented with a wider assessment of the role, this is done in a similar way but using key stakeholders. The stakeholders could be the CEO, a key member of the Leadership Team or an external independent third party, like a marketing NED on the board. In all cases the participating stakeholders need to think about what are the essential requirements for the marketing leader's role over the next 3 years.

When the self-assessment and role assessment are combined, the differences between the two provide further insights into how the marketing leader can be more effective. Having a good sense of who you are as a marketer and knowing the expectations from the CEO or another stakeholder is an important start for the marketer to advance. **There is power in knowing what you do not know.** It can reinforce where there is strong alignment, when you are working effectively with the Leadership Team and work increasingly becomes effortless. Conversely it can explain some of the frustrations or hot spot areas you or your CEO may be having which aren't being talked about and may become problem areas in the future.

The assessments are not a test. They are designed to make you, the marketers, think about how you operate now, what areas you excel in and enjoy. Similarly for the wider stakeholders it is an opportunity to get behind what is truly needed in the role. Both need to be answered as honestly as possible.

Taking the assessment is not essential. Many marketers and CEOs have found reading about ANCHOR Factors and the CODE helpful, either for them personally or to start a conversation about marketing.

Dip your toes in – the quick taster

The 12-question self-assessment is printed on the following pages. If you also want to carry out a stakeholder assessment, this questionnaire is at the end of the book.

In either assessment, read each statement and answer with a score of 1–5.

The scoring guide:

5 = Almost always
4 = Usually
3 = Sometimes
2 = Rarely
1 = Almost never

The scoring guide is the same for both the self-assessment and the stakeholder assessment.

The stakeholder assessment is focused on the role, so make sure the stakeholder doing the review does not think about you personally. There is no right or wrong, just write scores in the white box next to each statement.

	ANCHOR Factors Quick Self-Assessment (Part 1)	Answer (1–5)
Q1	Highly systematic and actively ensures there is clear prioritisation, governance and communication of projects and initiatives within the Leadership Team and across the wider business.	________
Q2	Data based decision maker, who deeply interrogates facts to make commercial decisions and, when relevant, understands the detail and benefits of new technology approaches.	________
Q3	Thrives on change, likes to work with the CEO on a change agenda, short cutting the existing approach and finding new solutions that are better for the business and customer.	________
Q4	Talented creatively, who ensures every customer touchpoint is a high quality experience and makes valuable imaginative leaps, which aren't always obvious to others.	________
Q5	Politically savvy and builds strong alliances across the Leadership Team, helps make progress by getting collective alignment and agreement to key tasks amongst the key leaders.	________
Q6	Optimisation expert focused on acquiring customers as cost effectively as possible, looks carefully at the customer journey and uses marketing techniques like direct response to drive conversion to sale.	________

Almost never	Rarely	Sometimes	Usually	Almost always
1	2	3	4	5

	ANCHOR Factors Quick Self-Assessment (Part 2)	Answer (1–5)
Q7	Challenging and forthright, sticks their neck out for what they believe in, brings truths to the Leadership Team which other people ignore, known for driving important debate within the Leadership Team.	______
Q8	Curious about customer needs and creates emotive propositions and multi-layer communication campaigns that make the brand/business highly relevant to the customer.	______
Q9	People-centric situational leader, who skilfully manages intercompany conflicts and makes everyone in the marketing team feel well supported, valued and aligned under a clear strategy.	______
Q10	Delivers the performance results that are needed, closely follows sales reporting and makes rapid tactical decisions to ensure the short-term targets are met daily, weekly or monthly.	______
Q11	Sets a high standard for the team to follow, rewards performance and promotes high performers, makes rapid decisions about under performance and boldly changes the organisational structure to deliver strategy.	______
Q12	Future focused, finds the most valuable future revenue streams and creates a coherent strategy and unifying clarion call for the business to follow.	______

Almost never	Rarely	Sometimes	Usually	Almost always
1	2	3	4	5

The scores then need to be transferred onto *The Marketing Leader's CODE*. There are specific positions for each question and score to be transferred to. The sector can be coloured-in between 1- 5 depending on the score you gave.

Question	**Position**	**Title**
1	1 o'clock	Consistency
2	4 o'clock	Analytical
3	7 o'clock	Change
4	10 o'clock	Creative
5	2 o'clock	Unity
6	5 o'clock	Conversion
7	8 o'clock	Challenge
8	11 o'clock	Connection
9	3 o'clock	Supportive
10	6 o'clock	Short-term
11	9 o'clock	Assertive
12	12 o'clock	Long-term

Self Assessment ☐
Role Assessment ☐

Self Assessment ☐
Role Assessment ☐

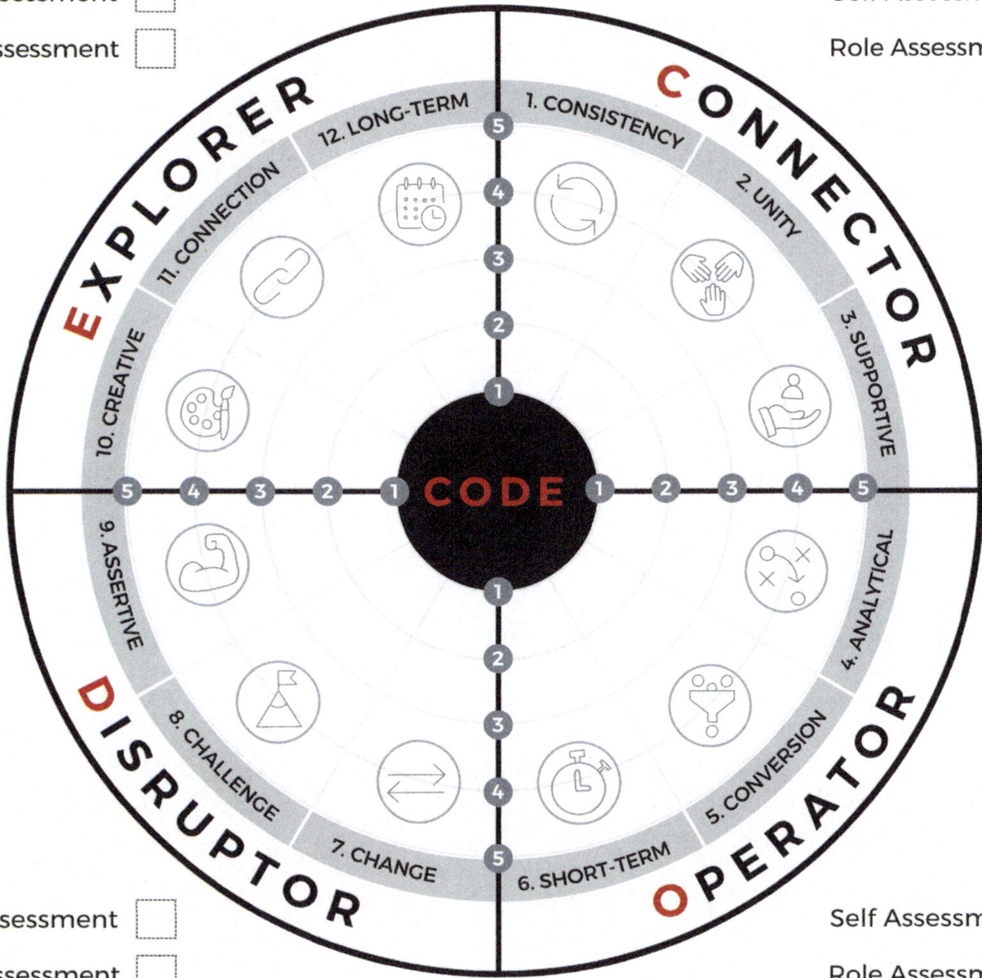

Self Assessment ☐
Role Assessment ☐

Self Assessment ☐
Role Assessment ☐

To work out your specific CODE, add up the scores in each quarter of the map or use the table below. Putting your totals in order, with the largest score first and the lowest last, will give you your CODE. Sometimes the scores may be the same for each letter of the CODE. It may well be the case that you are even across each genre, but if you want a more thorough assessment go to sideminds.com.

Connector	Operator	Disruptor	Explorer
Q1______	Q2______	Q3______	Q4______
Q5______	Q6______	Q7______	Q8______
Q9______	Q10_____	Q11_____	Q12_____
Total C_____	Total O_____	Total D_____	Total E_____

The same exercise can then be repeated with a stakeholder to assess the role and give it a specific CODE. Make sure they know they are assessing the needs in the role, not you! Transfer their scores in a similar way onto the *The Marketing Leader's CODE* using a different coloured pen.

CODEs, ANCHOR Factors and your results will be explained more in the next chapters.

PART 2: DISCOVER WHAT THE MARKETING LEADER'S CODE MEANS

ANCHOR FACTORS

In order to understand *The Marketing Leader's CODE* you need to start with understanding the 6 pairs of ANCHOR Factors. These are the behaviours and competencies that feed into 4 key genres called CODE: Connector, Operator, Disruptor and Explorer.

Every marketing leadership role and every marketer will have some of each of the ANCHOR Factor pairs. The emphasis will vary from role to role and marketer to marketer, with some having a higher bias towards one or the other of the pairs, or both. What is important is knowing which ANCHOR Factors you bring to the job and what the job is requiring. What is sacrosanct and essential, what is accepted as needing to evolve and change, and what areas have you genuine freedom to evolve and try out new things?

ANCHOR Factors

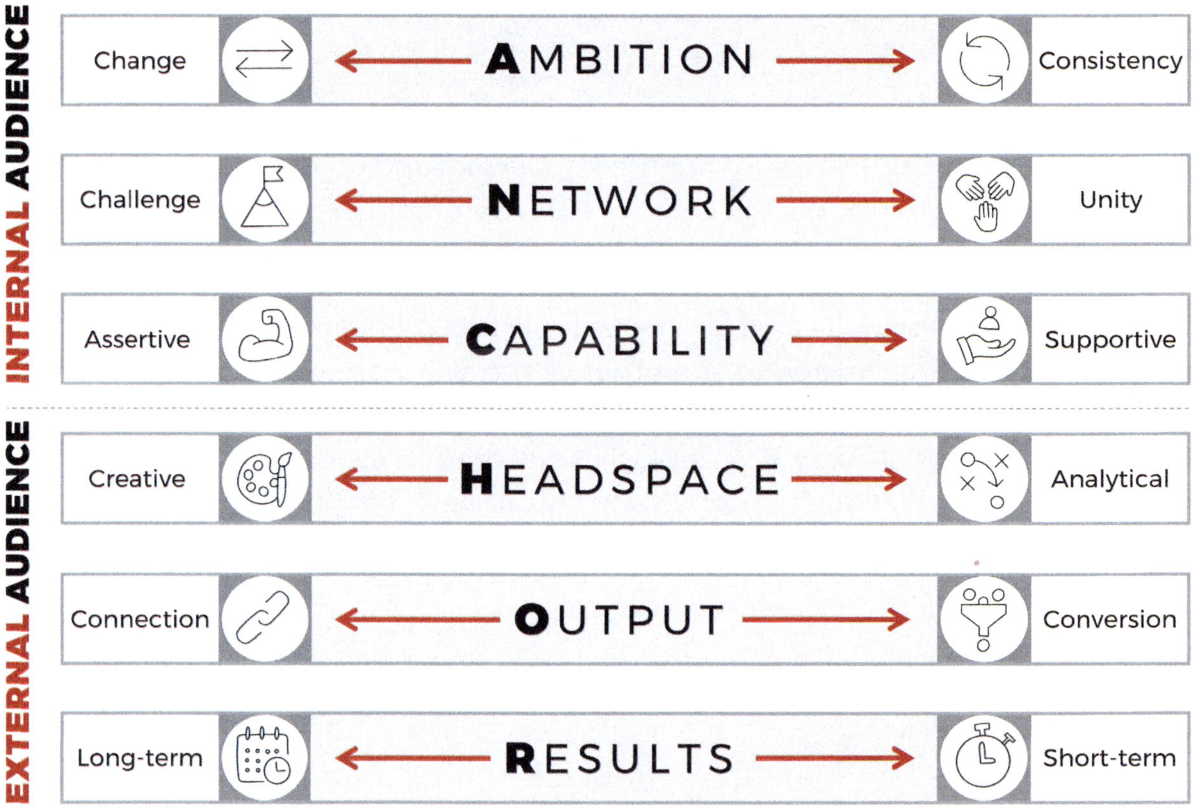

ANCHOR is not just an acronym for the 6 pairs of key behaviours and competencies. Metaphorically, if the business is a boat, then the marketer provides the stabilising anchor. The marketer finds the rich fishing grounds and then drops their anchor to hold the boat steady, so the Leadership Team with the crew can bring the fish onboard. As they do so, the marketer is assessing the weather, sea conditions, mood of the crew and competitors' boats all around. The boat will swing wildly and in opposite directions as conditions change, but a stable and strong anchor will hold the boat in position. This is just like the swing a marketer needs to manage on each ANCHOR Factor to keep the business focused on the customer and business growth.

AMBITION ANCHOR FACTOR

<table>
<tr><th>Change</th><th>← AMBITION →</th><th>Consistency</th></tr>
<tr><td colspan="3">AMBITION: Understands the natural homeostasis and works with the CEO to bring their business ambition to life and push the business forward. Tests new ideas and helps change areas which are sub-optimal and reinforces areas which need consistency.</td></tr>
<tr><td colspan="2">Change: Embraces the CEO change agenda and finds ways to rapidly test new approaches. Challenges the status quo, looks for shortcuts to historic procedures and evolves the way of working or working patterns. Encourages entrepreneurial thinking and finds intelligent ways to advance working practices and break up siloed thinking. Adapts quickly, responds to change easily and copes with obscurity. Sensitive to the external market.</td><td>Consistency: Establishes effective working practices with clear responsibility and decision-making. Gives individuals clarity on the areas they can operate freely and safely. Creates structures to keep stakeholders involved. Innovation is controlled and purposeful. Follows the business plan, monitoring progress and ruthlessly prioritises activity.</td></tr>
</table>

Every company will have its natural homeostasis. A regular pattern of working that maintains its overall equilibrium through the business style, systems and set of rules that everyone in the company follows. It is a pattern that is generated over time and the business and employees will have a tendency to always return to this natural equilibrium or way of working unless they are given new goals and the freedom to operate in a new system safely. On a boat this **equilibrium is really important and especially relied upon when conditions are rough and everyone needs to play their part.**

Natural homeostasis in business is a combination of the business's culture and purpose. People get used to the culture and build a muscle memory around how they behave. It can be hard to change. It keeps businesses running, and in companies like Apple or Dyson, encourages experimentation and learning. It can also be a contributing factor to disasters, like Boeing Max 737 in 2019-20.[1] The natural homeostasis leads to an unwillingness to challenge the senior leaders, which in turn leads to a series of safety issues being overlooked.

L. David Marquet,[2] a newly appointed captain of the nuclear submarine USS Santa Fe, writes about this in *Turn the Ship Around!* He took on what was reputably the worst ship in the US fleet and in the book observes how broken it was. The crew would try to follow whatever order he gave, even if it was an impossible task, no one questioned his command. He knew things had to change and introduced a new approach, which empowered the team and in time his ship became the finest in the US fleet.

Culture is however nothing without purpose. Purpose lifts the every day activity and directs the muscle memory to work at a higher level. It helps everyone understand the context they operate in and gives a framework to make decisions. As David Lewis, the CEO of Tesco[3] says in Will Greenwood and Ben Fennell's book *World Class*, it can make all the difference in challenging times like Covid '... all those years of saying that the purpose was our magnet north, and that if you make a decision with the purpose in mind then it will be the right decision, really paid off ... our people just got on and did the right thing.'

The Ambition ANCHOR Factor considers the business's homeostasis and CEO's plan. The CEO may be new or there may be external factors influencing the CEO's agenda and driving a need for change. It is important to get an early understanding and appreciation of both, so you know how to get things done, what is sacrosanct and which are the areas of change being talked about. A CEO will have a vision and narrative on which parts of the business working patterns should stay and go. The marketing leader has a key role to play in helping the CEO create this or support what an existing CEO has already planned. What are the quick tests you can do to help validate the plan and build the narrative? Bland and Osterwalder's *Testing Business Ideas*[4] has some great quick turnaround suggestions.

Microsoft's CEO Satya Nadella had the narrative 'mobile first, cloud first', Mastercard's CEO Ajay Banga 'kill cash' and Sony's CEO Kenichiro Yoshida 'bring kando back' (kando is Japanese for emotional connection), which I am sure benefitted from the support of a good marketer.

So what are the CEO's convictions and beliefs? What is on their agenda, which areas are they hoping you will protect and nurture and what will you challenge and change? Which best practices and governance systems need to endure and what areas need to change? This could be the speed of innovation, the business's overall agility, attitude to risk or M&A.

This means understanding the business's approach, embracing what matters to the CEO and appreciating where they are on their journey with the business, wider stakeholders and investors. Every CEO will be looking for organic growth but, if a larger corporation or private equity backed, they may be thinking about inorganic growth through M&A or bolt-on acquisitions. One or two big deals can catapult the business value and the CEO's reputation. The CEO could also be early or late in their tenure which could influence their attitude to risk, legacy and investment. The median tenure for a CEO is 5 years,[5] so are they planning a bold business move or playing it safe?

It is worth thinking about investors too. Is there a heavyweight single investor who really pulls the strings and steers the boat? And what is their agenda? Is the business private equity backed or a listed company? If private equity, then get into the private equity mindset. Orit Gadiesh and Hugh MacArthur[6] highlight simple lessons private equity tend to follow in a way that is more systematic, focused and aggressive than the practices found in most companies:

'Define the full potential; define the blueprint; accelerate performance; harness the talent; make equity sweat; foster a results-orientated mind-set'

If a listed company, what is the relationship and blend of short-term to long-term investors? For instance, Paul Polman KBE from Unilever was a great CEO who won the hearts and minds of the long-term investors and led a period of transformation in 2009, well ahead of the wider business world.

This ANCHOR Factor is understanding the company's culture and purpose, getting into the mind of your CEO and finding your place to make an impact by managing Change with Consistency.

Case study 1: Following the founder

I have had the good fortune to work with many great entrepreneurial leaders. From Richard Reed, Adam Balon and Jon Wright at Innocent Drinks to Graham Bosher and James Davidson at Tails.com, or Richard Harpin at HomeServe. One of the most memorable on the Approach ANCHOR Factor was Alex Chesterman OBE, the founder of LoveFilm, Zoopla, Cazoo and no doubt more great companies in the future.

He had a clear vision, operated at pace and had a strong view on the approach he wanted to be adopted. He had a programmatic approach to M&A and in my tenure with him he bought 10 different companies before the entire business was acquired by Silver Lake in 2018. This steady stream of deals shifted the marketing emphasis from carefully building one brand with one audience to multiple brands, with multiple audiences and importantly driving synergy and productivity between the businesses.

As he pressed his approach on the business, the Leadership Team needed to adjust our strategies and activities to reflect the present state and plan for the future. Keeping essential everyday business activity running but being flexible and adaptable with plans and resources, and regularly communicating with the teams, so whilst there was turbulence they understood the bigger plan. We all needed to align with the CEO and be able to live comfortably with the Change ANCHOR Factor.

Case study 2: Landing on Mars

ANCHOR Factors are consistent across companies but the emphasis on each ANCHOR Factor can differ from company to company. I found this when I moved from the entrepreneurial business of Innocent Drinks into the well-established Mars food business. I was brought in by the CEO as a change agent and I could well have landed on Mars.

I was given a challenging brief to make 'Mars more Innocent', challenging because Innocent biased heavily towards the Change ANCHOR Factor and there were over 40,000 colleagues in Mars following a tight system based upon the Consistency ANCHOR Factor. The CEO wanted to retain the consistency that had made Mars so successful, but needed to also bring in a new, faster and more nimble approach that challenged these systems.

With the support of the CEO and wider Leadership Team I started to understand the current approaches that made the organisation successful and looked for opportunities to deliver change. The opportunity came when we looked at price tiering in the dog food category and proposed the introduction of a price fighter brand.

The marketing team launched the challenger brand[7], Misfits, in an agile way. The normal 'lock and load' European innovation cycle usually required careful alignment and buy-in from multiple countries and would have taken over 2 years from concept to launch. Misfits was launched within 6 months and over a dozen years on the brand still exists and is doing well. The historic procedures and process were respected and the CEO was able to start to impact his change agenda. It was a small project that built trust and alignment with the CEO and Leadership Team and enabled a wide shift in project development in the future.

Notes

1. Edmondson, A. (May, 2019). Harvard Business Review. https://hbr.org/2019/05/boeing-and-the-importance-of-encouraging-employees-to-speak-up/
2. Marquet, D. (2015). *Turn the Ship Around!: A True Story of Building Leaders by Breaking the Rules*. Penguin.
3. Greenwood, W., and Fennell, B. (2021). *World Class: How to Lead, Learn and Grow like Champion*. Penguin.
4. Bland, J., Osterwalder, A. (2020). *Testing Business Ideas*. Wiley.
5. PwC. (2019). CEO turnover at record high; successors following long serving CEOs struggling according to PwC's Strategy & Global Study. PwC. https://www.pwc.com/gx/en/news-room/press-releases/2019/ceo-turnover-record-high.html/
6. Gadiesh, O., and MacArthur, H. (2009). *Lessons from Private Equity Any Company Can Use*. Harvard Business Press.
7. Morgan, A. (1999). *Eating the Big Fish. How Challenger Brands can compete against Brand Leaders.* Adweek Media.

NETWORK ANCHOR FACTOR

Challenge	← NETWORK →	Unity

NETWORK: Navigates the Leadership Team effectively and ensures the right discussions are held and the right activity gets done. Skilful at knowing when to challenge and when to create unity for the wider business benefit.

Challenge: Drives debate and discussion. Challenges other Leadership Team members fairly. Strong advocate for the customer and prepared to stick their neck out for what they believe. Seeks the best outcome and avoids mediocrity. High resilience and persistence. Knows the facts that matter and uses data smartly and in an unbiased way to make a point fairly and encourage a robust debate. Observes the overall project burden on the business and actively stops activity in order to speed up activity elsewhere. Ensures tough discussions are held and decisions made.	Unity: Builds trust and influence, establishing key relationships and alliances with the Leadership Team to get jobs done. Politically savvy and a strong team player, aligning with the Leadership Team for the company benefit. Does what is right for the wider company even if this sacrifices marketing activity. Constructively drives project prioritisation. Adept at noticing group bias and managing Leadership Team brinksmanship around strategy. Ensures discussions are brought to a conclusion, so clear unified messages are delivered to the wider business.

The marketing leader needs to be collaborative and build Leadership Team alliances, whilst also being challenging, demanding and always focused on the customer.

Collaboration can involve the whole Leadership Team, like setting strategy, prioritising company-wide activity, creating mutual focus for team resources and agreeing clear messaging for the wider business. It can be exclusively with the Chief Finance Officer on budgets, the Chief People Officer on resources and salaries, the Chief Operating Officer on delivering activity in stores or shelves etc, or the Chief Product Officer, where it is not just improving the day-to-day customer experience but holding firm to the macro vision, and **pushing for a 'minimum lovable product'**[1] **not just a viable product.**

At the same time the marketing leader has to be prepared to represent the customer and stick their neck out for what they believe is right. They need to be custodians of insight, identify trends and get the business to double down and act fast as information changes. This means being masterful storytellers and debaters, who eloquently present information in commercial terms the Leadership Team recognise and are resilient enough to cope with the push back challenges of a senior team.

Sometimes the Leadership Team will have overlapping objectives, but so often this is not the case and this can feed streams of individual siloed activity in separate teams. As companies scale the focus can also shift from external to internal drivers, making the business become increasingly distant from the customer. This is a tension which needs careful management, breaking up the Leadership Team silos and creating collaboration, whilst bringing the customer into these debates.

This means the marketing leader has to be involved in the humdrum of the everyday but also look at how the Leadership Team are operating as a group and how this cascades into the wider business. Calling out when there is discord or social bias starts to interfere with the group task. Members of the Leadership Team can take the easy route, agree with the highest paid, and avoid the difficult decisions. This is unfortunately programmed into our biology:

'A general "law of least effort" applies to cognitive as well as physical exertion...Laziness is built deep into our nature.' **Daniel Kahneman**[2]

This balance of Challenge and Unity ANCHOR Factors are described more by Patrick Lencioni in *The Five Dysfunctions of a Team.*[3] His model to me feels focused on negative team behaviour, but reversing his concept around creates:

Many of these behaviours require the whole Leadership Team to commit, but challenge is something the marketer is uniquely suited for, with their eyes on the customer and the business. They need to be able to open up the big debates and get decisions made, not kick the problems down the road. A combination of Challenge and Unity ANCHOR Factors and getting the Leadership Team working better has proven wider business impact on effectiveness.[4]

Discussions and decisions need to be made, so as Jeff Bezos said from Amazon[5]:

"If I drive us over a cliff ... you're as much at fault as I am."

Some marketers are comfortable doing this, but others struggle as they try to balance unifying with the Leadership Team and ensuring challenging debates aren't sidelined. They may be up against strong alliances which already exist in the Leadership Team and are expected to behave in a certain way, possibly adopting the style and approach of the previous marketer, which is never sustainable long-term. To be effective, the marketing leader needs to confidently manage challenging debates about the customer, the business, the wider environment or Leadership Team behaviours in the boardroom, and know they are also able to bring the Leadership Team together for the wider good of the company.

The company needs to see unity. Nobody on a boat wants to see the captain and his officers disagreeing. They want confidence and composure, with messages which are delivered clearly and consistently in mass and micro-broadcast. McDonald's were the masters of this. There was the internal audience and the franchisee audience and each were managed extremely carefully. For the big conferences with the latter, the Leadership Team were even trained in their presentation by actors because they recognised the leaders' energy and body language was as important as the message itself.

Case study 3: Being prepared to bet your job

I have worked for several digital marketplace businesses, from Zoopla on properties, to MoneySuperMarket on insurance products, uSwitch on energy services and Checkatrade on tradespeople. Marketplace businesses match customer demand to vendor supply in a sector and if they do this well can become hugely successful.

In one case, I joined an established Leadership Team, where the business was struggling. Marketplace businesses have a flywheel where supply and demand need to be carefully managed. There is no point having demand from customers if there is a lack of supply. This is a poor customer experience.

Facing this situation I wanted to get back to basics and understand what the barrier was, why was supply slowing and if this a macro market effect or something we had self-inflicted. I was lucky to have a strong CFO who had joined at the same time and between us we were able to start asking questions and interrogating research assumptions.

This revealed a high level of unconscious bias affecting decision-making, which clouded the interpretation of data. There were multiple factors at play, HIPPO or highest paid person opinion, sunk cost bias and confirmation bias, which distorted data interpretation (read more about bias in *Noise*[6]) and the Leadership Team had stopped challenging the facts and instead begun to follow the path of least resistance.

The CFO and I had a strong hypothesis on what needed to change and both of us were prepared to bet our jobs on it. We created a hypothesis and progressively carried out a series of research tests which showed this misinterpretation of data. This led to a watershed moment, when supply (or sales) was falling well behind budget projections. We needed to either stick with our plans or reset them. Backed with the new research and two of us prepared to bet our jobs on the information, we managed to get the Leadership Team to shift in favour of the new strategy. This led to a number of costly projects being stopped and an emphasis on adding back value. This not just had an impact on the business performance, but a positive shift in team engagement, as the wider business saw the executive team unify and refocus.

Betting your job isn't for everyone, but marketers need to be brave and I don't know any marketer who has been fired for being brave.

Case study 4: Super tankers can turn

Many people criticise McDonald's for all sorts of reasons. It could be the perceived health credentials of the food, or the impact of such a large company on the environment or animal welfare. Having led the UK and Ireland marketing and food team, I have got behind the scenes and have enormous respect for what they are trying to do, how they are responding to change and are leading the wider industry.

During my tenure the issue of single use plastic was increasingly becoming headline news. McDonald's already leads in many sustainability areas and had switched from plastic to paper straws, but still predominately used 'single use' plastic toys in the Happy Meal product. Changing this seemed like an impossible task. McDonald's was after all the world's largest manufacturer of toys and Happy Meal toy commitments were made years into the future.

The marketing team had concerns and were spurred on by the protest lead by two sisters Ella and Caitlin. They were two school girls who protested about plastic at our head office. I still remember the day they came in with their signed petition and hundreds of Happy Meal toys. This encouraged the marketing team to bring a series of proposals to the Leadership Team which involved switching from plastic to paper toys, introducing a toy recycling amnesty and letting customers switch toys for fruit bags. Old toys were even recycled into new playground equipment for charities.

This required a new supply chain, new in-store procedures and major toy stock write offs. The Leadership Team agreed to all the changes and the UK and Ireland were the first country in McDonald's to go plastic free in Happy Meal. It is possible to change the direction of a super tanker using Challenge and Unity.

Notes

1. de Haaff, B. (2017). *Loveability. How to build a business that people love and be happy doing it.* Greenleaf Book Group.
2. Kahneman, D. (2012). *Thinking, Fast and Slow*. Penguin.
3. Lencioni, P. (2002). *The Five Dysfunctions of a team*. Jossey-Bass.
4. Folkman, J. (2019). Extraordinary Leader 360-Degree Survey. ZengerFolkman.com https://zengerfolkman.com/wp-content/uploads/2019/08/EL360Survey_WP-2019.pdf
5. Rossman, J. (2014). *The Amazon Way: 14 Leadership Principles Behind the World's Most Disruptive Company*. Clyde Hill Publishing.
6. Kahneman, D., Sibony, O. and Sunstein, C. (2022). *Noise: A Flaw in Human Judgement*. Publisher. William Collins.

CAPABILITY ANCHOR FACTOR

Assertive ← CAPABILITY →	Supportive
CAPABILITY: Creates and maintains a high performing marketing team. Makes assertive decisions about the team and agencies and is a skilful situational leader, who is supportive and helps talent feel valued and grow.	
Assertive: Sets exacting standards, builds a high performing team and holds people and agencies to account. Confidently makes organisational changes to deliver strategy or key projects. Fairly raises the bar on performance and rewards delivery. Manages their own ego, backs high performers and is comfortable stepping back and empowering them with increased responsibility and opportunity. Clears the way with the wider Leadership Team to help the marketing team deliver their goals.	Supportive: Skilful situational leader who can assess and develop talent. Builds team capability and creates a strong team culture with everyone having a clear role and responsibility in delivering the business and marketing strategy. Keeps the team focused on key tasks and manages conflicts. A good listener and role model. Creates a safe environment that encourages learning and growth. An authentic leader, who can be trusted with a clear sense of purpose for the team.

The ANCHOR Factors of Approach and Network have so far been about upward and sideways influence and effectiveness in the Leadership Team. The Capability ANCHOR Factor is now about downward influence. The marketing team should be the powerhouse, who drive the business forward and the marketing leader needs to win their support and quickly have them pointing in the right direction, with clarity on roles and expectations.

The sooner marketing is a high calibre, focused, motivated and driven team, the sooner the marketing leader can get on with being the bridge with the wider business and making an impact. The marketer can do nothing until they have the team behind them.

The team needs to be quickly assessed to ensure the capabilities and organisation are aligned with the strategy. This needs to be done thoroughly and without bias or judgement, so you have the maximum diversity. This can be very challenging due to internal noise and unconscious bias, but you need to know who are the star employees, which jobs are the critical 10% that hold the real value creation in your team and get the right people in the right seats.

In the process you need to also look out for the culture champions. There is always a small number of people who contribute more than core performance numbers. They help set the tone and rhythm to the team and generally make people feel good. They remember birthdays, enthusiastically participate in events and are in-tune with the overall team morale.

It is the same with agencies. Long-term relationships can be highly successful, like McDonald's with Leo Burnetts, who have had a relationship for over 4 decades. The agency don't just deliver great work, but continuously live the values of McDonald's. For me this was most noticeable in Covid, where they were progressive, but showed empathy and humility. This sort of relationship is, however, very rare and it staggers me how agency performance can drop and this seems to be acceptable. The game of winning the account with the best people, slowly switching out the team to a more junior one and only bringing the top team back when the account needs to be rescued. In the same way as the marketing teams are managed and monitored, agencies' teams need to be tracked against targets, and not be allowed to drift along based upon reputation.

It is like the scene in Moneyball[1] where Billy Beane (Brad Pitt), ignores the bias of scouts and chooses a baseball team based upon performance (on a search engine of your choice, search for "Moneyball: science vs scouts") not misplaced reputation.

The marketing leader needs to be the supportive leader, who develops and nurtures key individuals, and the team culture. They also need to be assertive, setting high standards and firm on underperformance without penalising failure.

David Pottruck, the leader of Charles Schwab, the US trading and investment company says it all:

'The idea that failure is okay is ridiculous. I am not going to go around the company and reward someone for failing. But here at Schwab we differentiate between noble failure and stupid failure.'[2]

The team need to know you have got their back, will protect them from negative energy and support and grow them, but in return they need to know you have a standard and you expect the team to deliver against this. If this means failing they need to know this is fine, as long as they fail smart and quickly.

A good point to start reviewing the team is checking that marketing strategy and objectives are well defined and cascaded into the team. It surprises me how often the business strategy has not been translated into a marketing strategy with clear goals and outcomes that are regularly monitored. The business strategy and KPIs needs to be deconstructed into a marketing strategy and KPIs which are fed through to each marketing role. This is pivotal to setting budget, headcount and organisational design and making sure the right things get done. It is an old adage but what gets measured, gets done. Far too often business strategy jumps into marketing tactics and plans, which mean repetitive behaviours, incorrect KPIs and a strategy that is never delivered properly. Research from Harvard suggests that on average only 63%[3] of the financial performance strategies promised get delivered, because the strategy isn't translated properly into teams and execution, or as Henry Ford[4] said,

'If you always do what you've always done, you'll always get what you've always got.'

Customer strategic outputs need to be defined and, however painful this can be, the marketing leader needs to pivot the team organisation around this. Carrying people or agencies who do not fit the structure or are underperforming weighs down the marketing leader and affects performance in the long run.

Inaction with underperformers in your team sends out signals to marketing and the wider business.

The true performers in your team will have spotted these underperforming individuals already and only by addressing this do you remove roadblocks, ensure standards are met and recognise true talent. This does not mean dramatic clear-outs but sensitive and respectful change. Sometimes the least compassionate action is to leave a person in a role they aren't performing in. They lose energy, confidence and this can have wider implications on that person's overall well-being.

The marketing leader needs to show the Assertive and Supportive sides of the Capability ANCHOR Factor. Thomas Barta and Patrick Barwise's[5] empirical study of over 7,000 marketers and non-marketing leaders showed getting the marketing team mix right is the biggest impact of business success at 20%. As they say:

'You need the right mix of team skills, styles and personalities (including yours). To build a powerful tribe, align the team closely around a common goal.'

Case study 5: Masterful multitasking

One of the most impressive organisations who were on top of the Capability ANCHOR Factor were Money.co.uk, which I got to know in 2014 through acquisition. They were a relatively small online financial services comparison site which had approximately 2.5m visits a month and were highly profitable. The team was very small but highly effective. When I met them I imagined they would be burnt out, but far from it, they consistently ranked highly as one of the best places to work.

What made them so impressive on Capability was their fluid organisational structure. They relentlessly followed the Objectives and Key Results (OKR) goal-setting framework for running projects. This system developed by Andrew Grove[6] at Intel and later credited by Larry Page, the former CEO of Alphabet and co-founder of Google:

'OKRs have helped lead us to 10× growth, many times over. They've helped make our crazily bold mission of 'organizing the world's information' perhaps even achievable. They've kept me and the rest of the company on time and on track when it mattered the most'

The Money.co.uk OKR approach was aligned with a quarterly review process, where projects and resources were reset. Key projects which were stalling had resource reallocated to help them accelerate and although they were a small team they could uniquely do this because the team had become multitalented. The PR Lead, for instance, might also be a Project Manager and was being supported to learn programming code. Resource could be moved to where it was needed most and everyone had ownership of specific goal outcomes.

This approach would not work everywhere, but the team at Money.co.uk had adapted to the organisational challenges. This has made me recognise how important it is to have some flexible generalist resources in the marketing team, so resource can pivot to where it is needed.

Case study 6: Unifying teams

Capability was a key ANCHOR Factor when I was asked to go on secondment to Checkatrade, part of HomeServe. Checkatrade is the UK's largest online marketplace to find reputable tradespeople to carry out home repairs and maintenance. I was asked to be CMO and unify three distinct marketing teams.

There was the customer acquisition team, the tradespeople acquisition team and the tradespeople retention team. Each was effective in their own right, focusing on their own distinct objectives but had increasingly grown apart. KPIs weren't always aligned between the three areas, the brand had a subtly different look and feel, and roles had started to morph, stretch and overlap.

There was an opportunity to reorganise the team to make it more efficient and effective, but as the new CMO from central head office I could not simply go in and change things. I needed to get to know everyone personally, so quickly set up informal, agenda-less 121s with everyone. I wanted to get behind the potentially biased opinions, understand what everyone did and get to hear what they saw as opportunities and risks.

I was in listening mode, hearing their history, understanding what was and was not working and appreciating their points of view. You could start to see the star players who created value and time and again they also pointed out the problem areas. My task was to translate what I heard against the business strategy, identifying the critical roles, filling them with the star players, remove fringe or duplicating areas and give everyone a clear role down the marketing funnel.

This started to create a high performing team with a 'one team' attitude. The previously siloed system rewarded performance within one area, but meant the implications elsewhere in the marketing funnel were ignored. I needed the team to see their role more widely and care about the impact they had on others, so KPIs became not just about acquisition but retention too. Good team performance was rewarded, and siloed performance wasn't.

Notes

1. Lewis, M. (2003). *Moneyball: The Art of Winning an Unfair Game*. W.W. Norton and Company.
2. Jennings, J., and Haughton,L. (2007). *It's Not the Big that Eat the Small ... It's the Fast that Eat the Slow*". Harper Collins.[
3. Mankins, M., and Steele, R. (July- August, 2005). Turning Great Strategy into Great Performance. Harvard Business Review. https://hbr.org/2005/07/turning-great-strategy-into-great-performance
4. Ford, H. (unknown). www.thehenryford.org
5. Barta, T., and Barwise, P. (2017). *The 12 Powers of a Marketing Leader*. McGraw-Hill Education.
6. Grove, A. (1985). *High Output Management*. Random House USA Inc; 1st Vintage Books ed edition.

HEADSPACE ANCHOR FACTOR

<table>
<tr><td>Creative</td><td>← HEADSPACE →</td><td>Analytical</td></tr>
<tr><td colspan="3">HEADSPACE: Moves comfortably from using their left brain, full of data and detail, to their right, full of images, concepts and connections. Combines analytical skills with creative aptitude and flair.</td></tr>
<tr><td colspan="2">Creative: Turns business issues into creative opportunities. Uses data as a springboard for insight discovery, creativity and vision. Finds creative solutions to business issues that are not always obvious to others. Prepared to make creative leaps using experience. Makes every customer touchpoint a high-quality customer experience and has sound overall creative judgement. Inquisitive and curious, interested in customers, the wider market and the opportunities new technology can bring.</td><td>Analytical: Rigorously uses data and logic from multiple sources to inform decision-making. Keeps the company honest with its data and ensures marketing metrics are tied to business metrics everyone understands. Finds ways to enrich data and scenario test. Understands the pros and cons of new technology and how it could provide improved performance or generate new revenue streams. Interested in the detail and ensuring this is accurate and accessible.</td></tr>
</table>

How do you balance data, logic and technical acumen with insight, vision, and creative leaps based upon judgement and experience alone? Headspace is one of the most extreme factors for the marketing leader to master and in many ways makes the marketing role so unique and special.

As a marketing industry we are now able to analyse and assess activity better than ever. We can bring large sets of data together to understand behaviour and strategise possible solutions. Technology is transforming our relationship with customers, through data platforms, AI, content management and sophisticated attribution and modelling.

Marketers need to be comfortable not only in the data space and understanding the role of data and create logical fact-based answers, but also increasingly hold their own in technology discussions.

In Forrester's 2022 Predictions Report[1] they recognise two camps of marketing leaders:

'Some with the CMO title will continue to be side lined by the likes of another chief "something" officer — relegated only to the subset of marketing involving brand and promotion — while elite CMOs (those with data, martech, customer experience, and product chops) will capitalize on this moment in time to duly expand their remit.'

This will come to light more as we move from the mobile era of Web2 into the blockchain era of Web3. Web2 allowed us to read, write and share, and was the technology that enabled Twitter and Facebook. Web3 will create a new and better internet and change the way that consumers interact with brands. Consumers will be able to meet in new worlds, collaborate better, own digital assets and have a totally unique digital self. This whole new virtual world will have even more marketing channels and prospects for brands to operate. Marketing leaders need to be able to understand the core technology and encourage their team to experiment and find new relationships and revenues streams with consumers. As Henry Cowling[2] said:

'For marketers willing to reimagine the consumer relationship, Web3 offers new paths to growth.'

One of my last roles was in a digital business where we were going through an IT transformation programme to help the business become more responsive and nimbler. In marketing it changed our cloud data and content delivery systems and influenced multiple smaller projects, and the marketing leader needed to engage and understand this to be effective. You didn't need to be the expert, but had to appreciate the pros and cons, not just because of the benefits it should bring long-term, but the resourcing and cost implications in the short-term. Being at least semi tech-literate will I am sure be more significant for future marketers.

At the same time creativity remains king when it comes to campaign effectiveness. It is one thing to gather the data and another to interpret it and creatively leverage it into future focused initiatives that capture the customer's imagination and purchases. The work by Peter Field[3] shows campaigns awarded for their creativity are ten times more efficient. Creativity is after all the most beautiful way to solve a business issue.

To be successful, the marketing leader needs to be able to make creative leaps, underpinned by technical rigour and analysis. The marketer needs to be Creative and Analytical.

As data and analytics grow, companies are becoming more focused on performance metrics and creativity gets broken down into a series of small AB tests. Big ideas can evaporate and small, short-term financial metrics become more and more involved in decision-making to mitigate risk and look for certainty that doesn't exist. Instead there needs to be courage and speed, so a decision is made on incomplete information.

I recently met a CMO whose Chief Financial Officer had become the Chief of Economics, with responsibility bridging marketing planning, budgeting and performance and was engaged in the digital business model. It seemed a small change, but her alarm bells were ringing as the role increasingly encroached on her area and the company biased to analytics not creativity.

This change, I imagine, could accelerate. Whilst the marketing role has changed, the finance department in particular has changed too. It has shifted from being a transactional role, through to a broader planning and forecasting role, and then into managing M&A, the operating model and value management. Could the next obvious horizon be data, advanced analytics and potentially digital marketing? I hope not.

AI, big data, machine learning is all around us and it is only going to get more prevalent in our lives. This is all good, but alongside we need to find the place for creativity and imagination. As the marketing guru Mark Ritson[4] says:

'Creativity drives so much of effectiveness – and we've all forgotten it in the last decade. We now need to remember it for the decade that comes.'

Case study 7: Calculated risk taking

MoneySuperMarket was the number 2 online price comparison site in the UK. The business was performing well but the brand lacked traction with customers. It was well known but was not the first brand customers would think of when it came to switching car insurance. There needed to be a creative leap. I needed to win the CEO's and CFO's support to try something new and give them both confidence in the commercial return this would deliver.

This creative leap started with hard facts. The work of Les Binet and Peter Field[5], Byron Sharp[6] and John Phillip Jones[7] needed to build the investment case, alongside real-life econometric case studies by the likes of Gracie Kite.[8] This methodical approach focused on tangible case studies and results, established trust with the CEO and CFO and lead to the creation of the Epic Strut ad in 2015.

The final creative was risqué but as a marketing team we were confident it would work. The brand's awareness and reputation soared, and the advert became the UK's favourite ad of the year. The campaign went viral and on UK Budget Day, the front page of *The Sun*, the leading British Newspaper, even had the then Chancellor George Osbourne doing a pastiche of the Epic Strut.

This was flattery for the marketing team, but the campaign still needed to show it delivered leads and revenue to the CEO and CFO. Marketing metrics around brand searches and hurdle rates on advertising were turned into hard numbers, so creativity and analytics were delivered to the CEO and CFO.

Case study 8: Stay curious

In the humdrum of daily work we all get caught up in routine. The daily meetings, the regular reporting, the endless correspondence and stakeholder management to get things done. There is hardly enough time to manage all of this, let alone have an abstract hunch which might be valuable long-term. But these hunches are important. Marketing is about finding future revenue streams and this means staying curious.

I worked in the past on the breakfast cereal category. The market was pretty static and the major innovation was around kid's cereals and new guidelines around healthy eating. This was hardly the environment for a 100-year-old brand called Shredded Wheat. The primary audience was over fifties, who bought into the brand because it was natural and wholesome. It was after all 100% wheat and no added sugar and salt.

The brand was slowly declining and something needed to be done and a top-down decision was made to launch a kid's version called Sporties. This leveraged the brand's health credentials to target kids. The brand even had an iconic sports star at the time, Michael Owen, as the brand spokesperson and a uniquely designed 'power zone' inside each biscuit.

It was a disaster. Sporties was quickly redesigned and relaunched but it kept failing. Shredded Wheat was a substantial eat and, whilst the idea worked on paper with parents, it did not fly with kids. The common playground expression 'Never Eat Shredded Wheat' to teach kids the points of the compass (N-E-S-W) probably also did not help.

Around the same time the brand team were looking at how they could be more effective with their core audience, the over fifties. This audience were more health aware and bought Shredded Wheat because it was simple, honest goodness. The trouble was most of the benefits of the cereal were linked to the absence of ingredients. No added salt and sugar were important, but it is a little like saying no added cholesterol. The team therefore looked for alternative ways to promote the brand. Initially we started a partnership with the British Heart Foundation, donating over £250k per year. It was a natural partnership for the brand, but also ended up getting the company in court with Shropshire Trading Standards for misleading the customer on the brand's health benefits. This was not intentional, and energised the team to find a way to talk about the positive messages in a more constructive way.

By coincidence, epidemiological data and clinical studies were taking place in the US on whole grain. This was starting to show strong association between whole grain intake and a reduction in risk of coronary heart disease by up to 20–30%. The team's hunch had some substance and the studies were followed up. Cutting a long story short, Shredded Wheat was repositioned to heart health and in its first year grew 17%. All Nestle and General Mills cereals globally were subsequently positioned around their whole grain content, and whole grain became a new health benefit.

Notes

1. Forrester team. (October, 2021). Predictions 2022: CMOs Emerge as Emboldened Business Leaders. Forrester. www.forrester.com/blogs/predictions-2022-b2c-cmo-trends/
2. Cowling, H. (July, 2022). "The Business Case for Web3". The CMO Club Innovation Forum. https://thecmoclub.com/
3. Field, P. (2015). Creativity and Effectiveness with Peter Field. Thinkbox. www.thinkbox.tv/creative/insight/creativity-and-effectiveness-with-peter-field/
4. Ritson, M. (2020). Brand size, creativity main drivers of effectiveness. WARC. www.warc.com/newsandopinion/news/brand-size-creativity-main-drivers-of-effectiveness/43074
5. Binet, L., and Field, P. (2013). *The Long and the Short of It: Balancing Short and Long-Term Marketing Strategies.* Institute of Practitioners in Advertising.
6. Sharp, B. (2010). *How Brands Grow: What Marketers Don't Know*. Oxford University Press.
7. Phillip Jones, J. (January, 1990). Ad Spending: Growing Market Share. Harvard Business Review. www.hbr.org/1990/01/ad-spending-growing-market-share
8. Kite, G. (unknown). The Wrong and The Real of It. Magic Numbers. www.magicnumbers.co.uk/articles/the-wrong-and-the-real-of-it/

OUTPUT ANCHOR FACTOR

<table>
<tr><td>Connection</td><td>← OUTPUT →</td><td>Conversion</td></tr>
<tr><td colspan="3">OUTPUT: Focuses on priority audiences and effectively manages the marketing activity throughout the marketing funnel. From building a connection higher up the funnel, through to the conversion and retention lower down the funnel.</td></tr>
<tr><td>Connection: Creates long-term demand by developing a brand with a clear value proposition which is memorable, relevant and distinctive throughout the purchase journey. Uses mass market and mass personalisation digital and analogue media levers. Goes beyond the rational to build affinity and emotional connection, so the brand becomes a primary destination. Develops compelling retention programmes for different segments. Finds ways to reduce reliance upon short-term sales tactics and instead builds lifetime value.</td><td colspan="2">Conversion: Turns awareness and consideration into sales using effective direct response and optimisation techniques across multiple media channels. Understands different customers' buying journey and with the customer experience team optimises these journeys, so the customer is 'warmed up' with appropriate content and messaging. Works closely with the sales team to refine promotional offers and turn leads into sales. Carefully manages acquisition costs and maximises short-term return.</td></tr>
</table>

The range of marketing tactics grows every day. Owned, earned, shared, paid and traditional broadcast gives the marketer a blend of mass marketing and highly personalised performance activity to reach the customer.

In this diverse and changing world there tends to be two types of marketing leaders. Those who become the leader by predominately climbing the digital ladder, with more of a focus on conversion and targeted personalised digital marketing on customers lower down the marketing funnel, or those who climbed the brand ladder with a bias to connection and mass market brand higher up the funnel. This sometimes leads to the creation of two roles, the Chief Brand Officer and the Chief Digital Officer, or becomes unified under a Chief Marketing Officer. The choice is dependent upon circumstance and the required balance of Conversion and Connection.

My early career was with Unilever, Nestlé and Mars and was heavily biased to brand building and the Connection ANCHOR Factor. I enjoyed it, although had growing concerns I was becoming a marketing dinosaur and in 2012 switched from FMCG to E-commerce businesses to build my Conversion ANCHOR Factors, especially my performance and digital skillset. This career move did not increase my salary but was one of the best moves I ever made. This zigzag career step ensured I was able to deliver on both sides of this ANCHOR Factor as a marketing leader.

Balancing these two forms of marketing is an ongoing challenge for many marketing leaders. Long-term brand building and short-term activation ideally needs to be 60/40[1] but getting to this balance can be hard. Marketing investment can be seen as a cost centre and not a revenue generator if not presented clearly. An attitude which can lead to increasingly short-term behaviour which can be hard to shake off. Getting CFOs or CEOs to hold their nerve on resetting the balance is very difficult.

In several companies I have joined we have started this journey towards increased brand building, but the long-term effects are slow to realise and often these journeys are curtailed. Putting the creative performance aside, this usually comes down to one of three internal issues:

Leadership Team support: It is essential to have the Leadership Team aligned and supportive to the investment return and KPIs over a longer time frame. This means a well forecast plan that is prudent and not over bullish, which shifts away from short-term metrics like cost per lead metrics into engagement and overall lifetime value. If this cannot be agreed you should stop – over optimistic plans will put you on the back foot and until you get this agreement you should stay focused on short-term conversion optimisation.

Wider company involvement: The campaign needs to be aligned early with other departments and, when relevant, integrated into development roadmaps. A lack of engagement with key teams can undermine brand building activity if the sales team aren't fully involved with new sales messages, or for tech businesses, the product team haven't evolved the customer journey or landing pages. There can be unexpected consequences that need to be thought through. Everyone has to be onboard and a sequential plan put in place to test, learn and roll-out.

Appropriate investment: There are many ways to engage customers and build a brand. Too often businesses still rely upon mass market media, but there are more affordable and measurable steps that can be done first. Small tests can prove critical hypotheses and these can then be built together into a logic stream for a wider roll-out. The customer rarely acts upon one piece of communication but will have multiple contact points through multiple media before they make a purchase. Test out the easier, affordable channels first, before rolling out into mass marketing activity that delivers across the marketing funnel.

Case study 9: Building a brand

One of my most rewarding marketing journeys was with Tails.com, an online home delivery subscription service for personalised pet food. Like all start-ups, customer demand started by building a sound foundation, through SEO partnering with the tech and product team and subsequently introducing performance media and PR. The team then tested, learnt and rolled out new activity like partnership, affiliates, inserts and find-a-friend. The approach was sequential, methodical, and all the time three things held true:

- The brand had clear distinctive design assets that were consistently deployed across all touchpoints,
- The customer journey from each communication was thoroughly assessed before going live, to ensure conversion was optimised,
- Decisions were made with data and an objective view was made on every channel's cost per acquisition.

The approach evolved and started to include traditional broadcast, initially with Direct Response TV and other high dwell direct response mechanisms like tube car panels. SEO built momentum with increased focus on load speed, content and user experience. With success broadcast media expanded, shifting from rational Direct Response TV to more emotional brand messaging and widening the reach to light users. A journey of Conversion and Connection both being embraced and optimised. Tails.com was subsequently sold to Nestlé.

Case study 10: All things communicate

A memorable experience in optimising the customer's experience with the brand was in developing Bear Snacks. I teamed up with Andrew and Hayley Gait-Golding who were importing dried fruit into the UK and were keen to develop a healthy brand for kids. We looked at the options available and honed in on Kellogg's Winders, marketed as a playful brand for kids but there were 12 different ingredients and most of them incomprehensible. There had to be a healthier version, something that was as tasty as a chocolate bar and healthy as fruit.

Hayley was a fruitarian, knew everything about fruit and was sure she could create something as playful as a Winder, but with one ingredient. Fruit. Well to be honest two, fruit and sometimes veg.

The concept evolved and I brought in B&B Studio, a new design agency where we were Shaun and Kerry's first clients. With them we created Bear Snacks on a shoestring budget.

With such a tight budget we needed to make sure everything communicated. From business cards to sales invoices and secret messages kids could discover on the packaging. Everything was a potential connection point with a new customer and we wanted to be memorable, distinctive and talked about.

Our best connection point was, however, created by mistake. The fruit snack comes as pairs of fruit rolls which were originally simply packed in a wrapper side by side. The rolls slight stickiness meant they kept falling out of line and this stopped production. We needed to introduce a backing card to hold them in place. Every card squeezed the already delicate margins but we had no choice and decided to make these into collector cards with fun animal and fruit facts for kids to collect.

We never anticipated the impact the cards would have. They became trading currency at schools and combined with a simple fruit message gave us permission to talk to adults and kids through social media. Slowly the brand fame grew and marketing activity advanced. Even now there are collector sites for the cards[2] and eBay has sales of the cards taking place every day.

Notes

1. Binet, L., and Field, P. (2013). *The Long and the Short of It: Balancing Short and Long-Term Marketing Strategies.* Institute of Practitioners in Advertising.
2. www.yoyobearcards.co.uk

RESULTS ANCHOR FACTOR

<table>
<tr><th>Long-term ← RESULTS</th><th>RESULTS → Short-term</th></tr>
<tr><td colspan="2">RESULTS: Vigilantly monitors performance in year and responds with short-term initiatives to boost performance. Looks for future revenue opportunities and develops the long-term plan with key stakeholders.</td></tr>
<tr><td>Long-term: Engages and aligns the Leadership Team in the development of a long-term plan with clearly defined goals and growth opportunities. Keeps these goals front of mind within the Leadership Team through establishing quarterly company targets. Defines long-term ways to build value (innovation, M&A) and the marketing rules to win in key markets. Balances long-term and short-term performance metrics. Creates a compelling clarion call and story for the business and investors.</td><td>Short-term: Assesses short-term sales performance and market indicators. Gets to the root cause of performance and responds quickly. Accelerates activity which is working and adapts activity to gap fill. Street fighter attitude who finds tactical opportunities. Reviews pricing, ranges and promotional strategies. Focuses effort on highest returning activity to deliver the annual plan. Tests new channels for new sales and rapidly adjusts activity depending on costs and performance.</td></tr>
</table>

The marketing leader needs to be results-orientated, both in the long term as a strategic evangelist and short term as a savvy street fighter. They need to engage the Leadership Team in the long range plan, stay focused on where the customer is going and have a clear customer vision for the future. At the same time, they must be prepared to be a 'scrapper', understanding the customer experience online, in-store or on the street, getting into the detail of weekly sales and evaluating short-term tactics.

The marketing leader needs to have both a short-term and long-term results ANCHOR factor, with the CEO and Leadership Team regularly informed on the tactical activity to deliver the short-term alongside a planned approach to engage them in the long-term strategy.

Short-term issues can be symptomatic of a wider issue and if the marketing leader is going to have credibility with the leadership team, they need to show they know what is going on now. This means getting out on the street, regularly reviewing the online user experience, staying close to the sales team, hypothesising what is happening and coming up with a plan.

If things are going well, how can you open the taps and accelerate? If things are going badly, what needs to change quickly?

Thomas Barta and Patrick Barwise[1] call this 'Fall in Love with Your World' and 'Walk the Halls', and in their study were the second and third biggest impacts the marketer could have on the business at 18% and 13% respectively:

'Fall in Love with Your World: As a marketing leader, you really need to know your stuff (customers, products and industry)'.

'Walk the Halls: As a marketer, you won't change the world by sitting at your desk. You have to go out and engage people and making things happen'.

A new CEO who joined one of the HomeServe businesses did this brilliantly. He went through the online customer journey again and again with the marketing team, challenging why certain steps needed to exist and finding ways to enhance conversion and improve results. This scrutiny enhanced conversion by 30% and unlocked wider systemic issues. This was him doing seagull dive bombs on the team to get them to be more focused in this area. It should have been the marketing leader that did this.

Short-term tactics need to be carefully defined, so they do not undermine the long-term plan. The annual plan must be delivered, but investors want to see balance. Hit the short-term numbers but ensure the core long-term metrics and strategy is cohesive and clear.

Often the short term can become an increasing distraction. Future years become over optimistic turnarounds that do not address the core issue and performance doesn't materialise. On board a boat if the prevailing conditions don't shift there will be one optimum navigational course and way to set the sails. Unless you do something bold and different you will keep sailing in this direction. It is the same in business. Hockey stick growth is not achievable or sustainable unless the core issue is addressed.

Long-range strategy needs to be built with solid foundations, so the business can plan accordingly and stakeholders internally and externally understand the ambition. Mars was masterful at this with a thorough external audit of customer and shopper trends, and internal assessment of their capability and competitiveness. The process was rolled up into a plan that gave every business a clear focus and foundation.

Case study 11: Rule of 5

In most of the customer-centric businesses I have been in, the long-term plan has predominately been led by Marketing and been a combination of top-down objective setting and prioritisation from the Leadership Team, with bottom-up assessment and strategic recommendations from business teams.

Innocent Drinks had a particularly strong approach. The business was still privately owned and growing fast across Europe. Richard, Jon and Adam had one key principle above all others and that was to 'create a business we can be proud of'. The so-called 'Rocking Chair Test'.[2]

This principle filtered into clear company values (which are still at Innocent today), a vision to be 'Europe's favourite little drinks company' and a clear 5-year revenue goal. But as a team we were barely 100 people and there were so many things to do.

We had to make choices and ruthlessly prioritise. Defining where we were today, where we wanted to be in the future and stack rank activity so we focused only on the areas which would make the biggest impact. This meant saying no to opportunity after opportunity. In the end we had 5 big initiatives which everyone's personal objectives connected back to. Importantly it was only 5, the so-called rule of 5. This kept everything simple and clear.

This approach can be applied to every business. There is not necessarily a magic number 5, but every company can keep it simple. Even in large global companies like McDonald's we managed to boil the whole plan down to under 10 initiative themes.

Case study 12: Detail matters

McDonald's are the masters of operations and meticulous with detail. Seconds matter so they try to ensure every store gets it right first time. Of course there can be odd mistakes, but the team are constantly looking for ways to make short-term efficiency adjustments.

This eye for detail is drilled into everyone and as a new member of the business I spent my first week in-store working every station and getting to know the crew. It was a true eye opener and I have huge respect for all the McDonald's team.

My operations leadership peer was in particular impressive. We had regular leadership safaris in-store and on the street. This was to assess what we were doing well and badly, but also to see what could be optimised to attract customers in-store or into the driveway.

Detail mattered. How clear were the menu boards to read? Had we the optimum outdoor signage in proximity to store? Were helmeted Uber Eats or Just Eat delivery drivers intimidating customers? Was the right product being advertised at the right time of day? How competitive were our prices vs a new deal from a competitor? We needed to be constantly agile and responsive despite serving 3.5m customers every day. Simple questions that should be asked every day whatever the business size.

This led to some simple but effective activity which enhanced sales. From copying artisan coffee shops and introducing an A-frame menu board to disrupt the customer walking by, or in key high streets getting the team guerrilla couponing in the shoulder period between breakfast and lunch, and most importantly listening to customers. Why, for instance, should breakfast need to finish at 10.30 a.m.? This had always been the case for McDonald's in the UK and Ireland, but the social media disappointment of arriving 5 minutes late was palpable. Changing this to 11 a.m. substantially improved sales whilst still proving enough time for the staff to change over and prepare for lunch.

@ilovebrands

Waking up after a night out and realising you've missed McDonald's breakfast is just the worst.

Notes

1. Barta, T., and Barwise, P. (2017). *The 12 Powers of a Marketing Leader.* McGraw-Hill Education.
2. Germain, D. (2009). *A Book About Innocent: Our Story and Some Things We've Learned.* Michael Joseph.

THE MARKETING LEADER'S CODE

The 6 pairs of ANCHOR Factors can be grouped into 4 marketing genres – Connector, Operator, Disruptor and Explorer or CODE for short. There are 3 ANCHOR Factors for each, with the grouped ANCHOR Factors each having similar traits.

Every marketing leader and every role will have a little of each. What is important is to see if any areas are particularly high or low. Is there a clear sequence and bias? Do you lead with Connector and are a C-O-D-E, lead with Disruptor and are a D-E-O-C, or do you score evenly across all the different quadrants? There could be 24 different variations:

Connector led	Operator led	Disruptor led	Explorer led
CODE	OCDE	DCOE	EDOC
COED	OCED	DCEO	EDCO
CDEO	ODCE	DEOC	ECDO
CDOE	ODEC	DECO	ECOD
CEOD	OEDC	DOEC	EOCD
CEDO	OECD	DOCE	EODC

The CODE is how you would naturally like to operate in a business. If this is perfectly aligned with the business needs, you'll be operating at your best and will be most effective in the Leadership Team. The role could, however, have a different CODE and you need to behave differently. Unless you know this, the chances are you and your team could be underperforming.

Your CODE will evolve and change as your experience grows and develops. Similarly the CODE for a role can change over time and will be different for one marketing leadership role to another. This can help sometimes demystify the differences between the Chief Marketing Officer, Chief Digital Officer, Chief Growth Officer, Chief Customer Officer, Chief Brand Officer and Strategy Officer, as explained in the next section.

A little like Myers-Briggs your CODE will, to some extent, be influenced by your personality. You may find you are naturally heavily biased to the Operator genre, with a strong focus on analytics, conversion and short-term results and the opposing Explorer genre of creativity, connection and long-term brand building just is not you. This gives you a few options. Stay focused in the area you enjoy and look for jobs that focus primarily on this genre, or look at your team and think about how you bring this skillset in to compliment yourself. I have personally always been stronger in Explorer vs Operator. I've built up my skills as an Operator, but its not my strength and I've always looked to have strong Operator's as my number 2 supporting me.

CONNECTOR LED MARKETING LEADERS

Marketing leaders with Connector as their lead genre form very close relationships with the CEO, Leadership Team and wider business. They are skilful managers of the marketing team and are great at developing talent and building a strong marketing culture. They are good at adopting and following business processes and use internal expertise effectively.

These are the core behaviours of a Chief Marketing Officer in more established businesses and PLCs like Mars and McDonald's. They create close working relationships and partnerships beyond the marketing team.

Often promoted from within the organisation, they are well-networked internally and create unity and alignment across the Leadership Team. They understand the importance of getting internal alignment and buy-in, and create the alliances to make things happen.

The downside of being strong in this area can be a lack of external context. Connectors know how to operate internally in their business but often can need external advisers and agencies to help them retain a wider perspective. They might need to bring external capability into their team to counterbalance their own skills.

The Connector and Disruptor typologies are often linked to the business's stage of development. Connector typologies tend to come from larger companies, where alignment and integration is essential. Disruptors are likely to come from start-ups, where business processes are developing and shortcuts are taken at speed for competitive advantage.

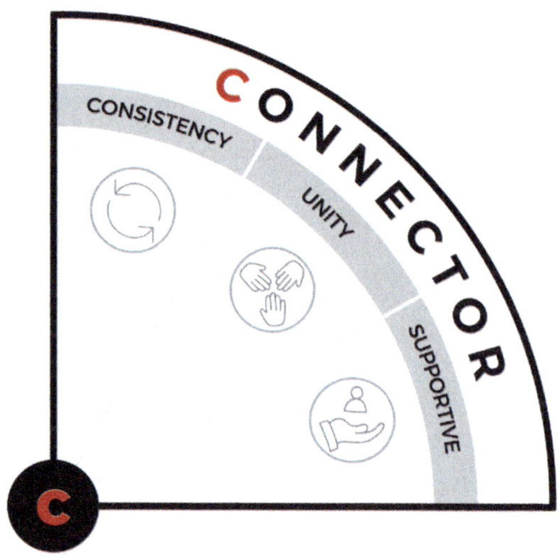

Consistency	Establishes effective working practices with clear responsibility and decision-making. Gives individuals clarity on the areas they can operate freely and safely. Creates structures to keep stakeholders involved. Innovation is controlled and purposeful. Follows the business plan, monitoring progress and ruthlessly prioritising activity.
Unity	Builds trust and influence, establishing key relationships and alliances with the Leadership Team to get jobs done. Politically savvy and a strong team player, aligning with the Leadership Team for the company benefit. Does what is right for the wider company even if this sacrifices marketing activity. Constructively drives project prioritisation. Adept at noticing group bias and managing Leadership Team brinksmanship around strategy. Ensures discussions are brought to a conclusion, so clear unified messages are delivered to the wider business.
Supportive	Skilful situational leader who can assess and develop talent. Builds team capability and creates a strong team culture with everyone having a clear role and responsibility in delivering the business and marketing strategy. Keeps the team focused on key tasks and manages conflicts. A good listener and role model. Creates a safe environment that encourages learning and growth. An authentic leader, who can be trusted with a clear sense of purpose for the team.

OPERATOR LED MARKETING LEADERS

Marketing leaders who have Operator as their lead genre tend to be more analytical and data led, with a strong skill set in performance media, sales conversion and short-term action. They are focused on campaign optimisation lower down the marketing funnel, where there is some category buying intent with customers, and creates strong partnerships with the sales team.

This focus on data, conversion and short-term impact is important to get a business established, but in the case of online businesses, can lead to the constant need to inefficiently reacquire customers again and again. Successful acquisition of consumers in new online businesses relies upon a great page ranking and this is highly influenced by competitor spend and the algorithm of Google, Facebook etc. You have to believe your onsite customer experience and retention tools are so outstanding that customers will decide to come direct in the future. Sometimes this works, but more often I find the marketing leader needs to have a strong Operator genre initially and then develop the Explorer genre, building expertise in long-term brand building and retention with, for instance, the recruitment of a Brand Director.

A marketing leader who has a strong score in this area is often biased to jobs like a Chief Digital Officer or a Chief Growth Officer, where performance-led acquisition and short-term results are key.

In some businesses there can be Chief Growth or Digital Officers alongside Chief Marketing or Chief Brand Officers. This I have found mainly occurs when there are two audiences, one which is a B2B audience and another B2C. The B2B audience may need a greater focus on sales promotion, creating a Chief Growth Officer role, whilst the B2C may have a blend across the whole marketing funnel and be more of a Chief Marketing Officer.

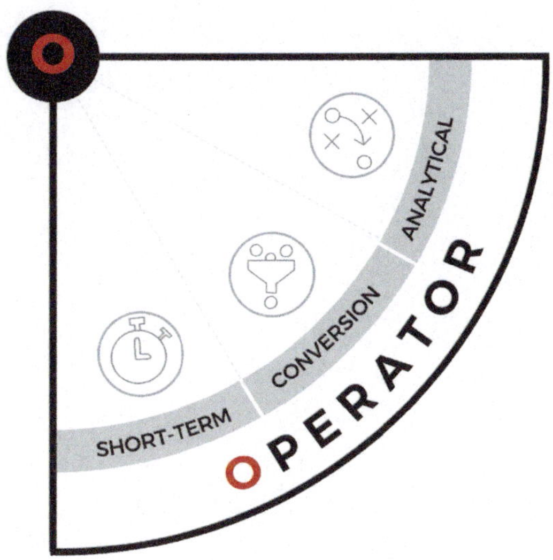

Analytical	Rigorously uses data and logic from multiple sources to inform decision making. Keeps the company honest with its data and ensures marketing metrics are tied to business metrics everyone understands. Finds ways to enrich data and scenario test. Understands the pros and cons of new technology and how it could provide improved performance or generate new revenue streams. Interested in the detail and ensuring this is accurate and accessible.
Conversion	Turns awareness and consideration into sales using effective direct response and optimisation techniques across multiple media channels. Understands different customers' buying journey and with the customer experience team optimises these journeys, so the customer is 'warmed up' with appropriate content and messaging. Works closely with the sales team to refine promotional offers and turn leads into sales. Carefully manages acquisition costs and maximises short-term return.
Short term	Assesses short-term sales performance and market indicators. Gets to the root cause of performance and responds quickly. Accelerates activity which is working and adapts activity to gap fill. Street fighter attitude who finds tactical opportunities. Reviews pricing, ranges and promotional strategies. Focuses effort on highest returning activity to deliver the annual plan. Tests new channels for new sales and rapidly adjusts activity depending on costs and performance.

DISRUPTOR LED MARKETING LEADERS

Marketing leaders who have Disruptor as their lead genre tend to be more entrepreneurial leaders who are opportunistic and thrive on change. They are externally focused and bring in fresh ideas. They tend to be very assertive with the team, rapidly changing the team shape to the situation at hand. They may have come from a strong start-up background and follow agile procedures. Innocent Drinks in the early days encouraged this approach from the founders downwards.

A marketing leader who has a strong score in this area might be a Chief Marketing Officer in a start-up or have a strong customer agenda and be biased to roles like a Chief Customer Officer.

Disruptor marketers are outward thinking and truly customer-centric. This can mean they also take accountability for the product development and innovation, or in digital businesses the customer experience on the site.

Disruptor led marketers have the customer's interest at heart and need to build strong partnerships with the Leadership Team to turn these ideas into action. Their approach and thinking can be transformational, but in the wrong company can jar with strongly established procedures.

Disruptors need the close alignment and support of the CEO and wider leadership. A disruptor in one business will not necessarily be a disruptor in another. It is important to understand what are the guardrails so you can be effective. In Mars I was brought in as a Disruptor, but I would never have seen myself as a Disruptor in Innocent Drinks. I was then only able to be successful in Mars with careful mentoring from the CEO.

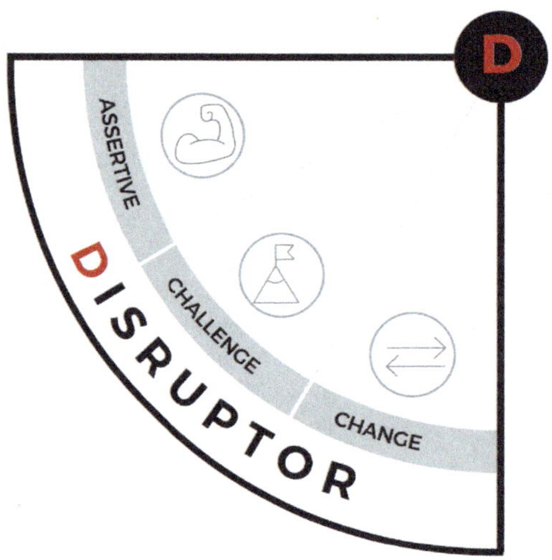

Change	Embraces the CEO change agenda ands finds ways to rapidly test new approaches. Challenges the status quo, looks for shortcuts to historic procedures and evolves the way of working or working patterns. Encourages entrepreneurial thinking and finds intelligent ways to advance working practices and break up siloed thinking. Adapts quickly, responds to change easily and copes with obscurity. Sensitive to the external market.
Challenge	Drives debate and discussion. Challenges other Leadership Team members fairly. Strong advocate for the customer and prepared to stick their neck out for what they believe. Seeks the best outcome and avoids mediocrity. High resilience and persistence. Knows the facts that matter and uses data smartly and in an unbiased way to make a point fairly and encourage a robust debate. Observes the overall project burden on the business and actively stops activity in order to speed up activity elsewhere. Ensures tough discussions are held and decisions made.
Assertive	Sets exacting standards, builds a high performing team and holds people and agencies to account. Confidently makes organisational changes to deliver strategy or key projects. Fairly raises the bar on performance and rewards delivery. Manages their own ego, backs high performers and is comfortable stepping back and empowering them with increased responsibility and opportunity. Clears the way with the wider Leadership Team to help the marketing team deliver their goals.

EXPLORER LED MARKETING LEADERS

Marketing leaders who have Explorer as their lead genre are strategic, insightful and brand-led and look at longer-term growth. These people could have been management consultants, planners in an advertising agency or have a more traditional mass market background. They thrive in developing business vision, M&A plan, brand strategy and customer value propositions.

A marketing leader with a strong score in this area has a brand and long-term strategy bias, they can often be called Chief Strategy Officer or Chief Brand Officer.

These marketers are focused more on the long term and are used to KPIs which reflect this. This means they can struggle with delivering shorter-term targets and goals, and need to ensure they have the right people in the team around them focused on the short term.

In one business I advised, they split the Chief Marketing Officer role and recruited one person strong in the Explorer genre (Chief Brand Officer) and one person who was strong in the Operator genre (Chief Digital Officer). This meant they had expertise in both areas, but this required the two to work together on the short-term and long-term investment cases. This was not always easy, which put pressure on the CEO.

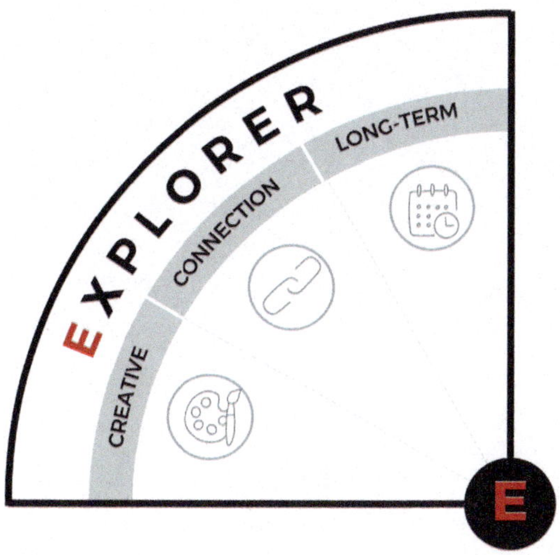

Creative	Turns business issues into creative opportunities. Uses data as a springboard for insight discovery, creativity and vision. Finds creative solutions to business issues that are not always obvious to others. Prepared to make creative leaps using experience. Makes every customer touchpoint a high-quality customer experience and has sound overall creative judgement. Inquisitive and curious, interested in customers, the wider market and the opportunities new technology can bring.
Connection	Creates long-term demand by developing a brand with a clear value proposition which is memorable, relevant and distinctive throughout the purchase journey. Uses mass market and mass personalisation digital and analogue media levers. Goes beyond the rational to build affinity and emotional connection, so the brand becomes a primary destination. Develops compelling retention programmes for different segments. Finds ways to reduce reliance upon short-term sales tactics and instead build lifetime value.
Long term	Engages and aligns the Leadership Team in the development of a long-term plan with clearly defined goals and growth opportunities. Keeps these goals front of mind within the Leadership Team through establishing quarterly company targets. Defines long-term ways to build value (innovation, M&A) and the marketing rules to win in key markets. Balances long-term and short-term performance metrics. Creates a compelling clarion call and story for the business and investors.

PART 3: USING THE MARKETING LEADER'S CODE

INTERPRETING YOUR RESULTS

In this section we will look at what your scores mean and what you can do about them. To make this section more practical, I will look at 4 different scenarios:

- Understanding your CODE
- Enhancing your Leadership Team impact
- Recruiting or onboarding a new marketing leader
- Becoming a future marketing leader

Once you have interpreted your results, each ANCHOR Factor in the next section is broken down into tools and tactics you can try to help boost your skills in each area.

Understanding your CODE

This looks at your self-assessment results only. To get started, ask yourself some questions:

- Which ANCHOR Factors are you scoring high and low? Are your low areas important to the business or not? Is someone else in the team covering these areas for you? Do these low scores matter?
- Are there any areas which seem to be a repeat niggle from the CEO or Leadership Team? Is anyone a seagull dive bombing you in one area which might be a key concern for them?
- How well aligned do you feel your profile is to the business's goals over the next 3 years? Are there gaps you feel you need to develop or do you have these covered by someone else in the team?

- What is your CODE and how well do you think this aligns with what you think the business needs? Which lead genre do you think suits the business – a Connector, Operator, Disruptor or Explorer?

In the example below, the marketing leader's CODE was Explorer led (E-C-D-O). They were strong in many of the ANCHOR Factors and their assessment showed their 'Operator' genre and related ANCHOR Factors were weaker. A gap like this is not unusual but in this case the business was going on a digital transformation. It is a similar profile to the one I had soon before switching into digital e-commerce.

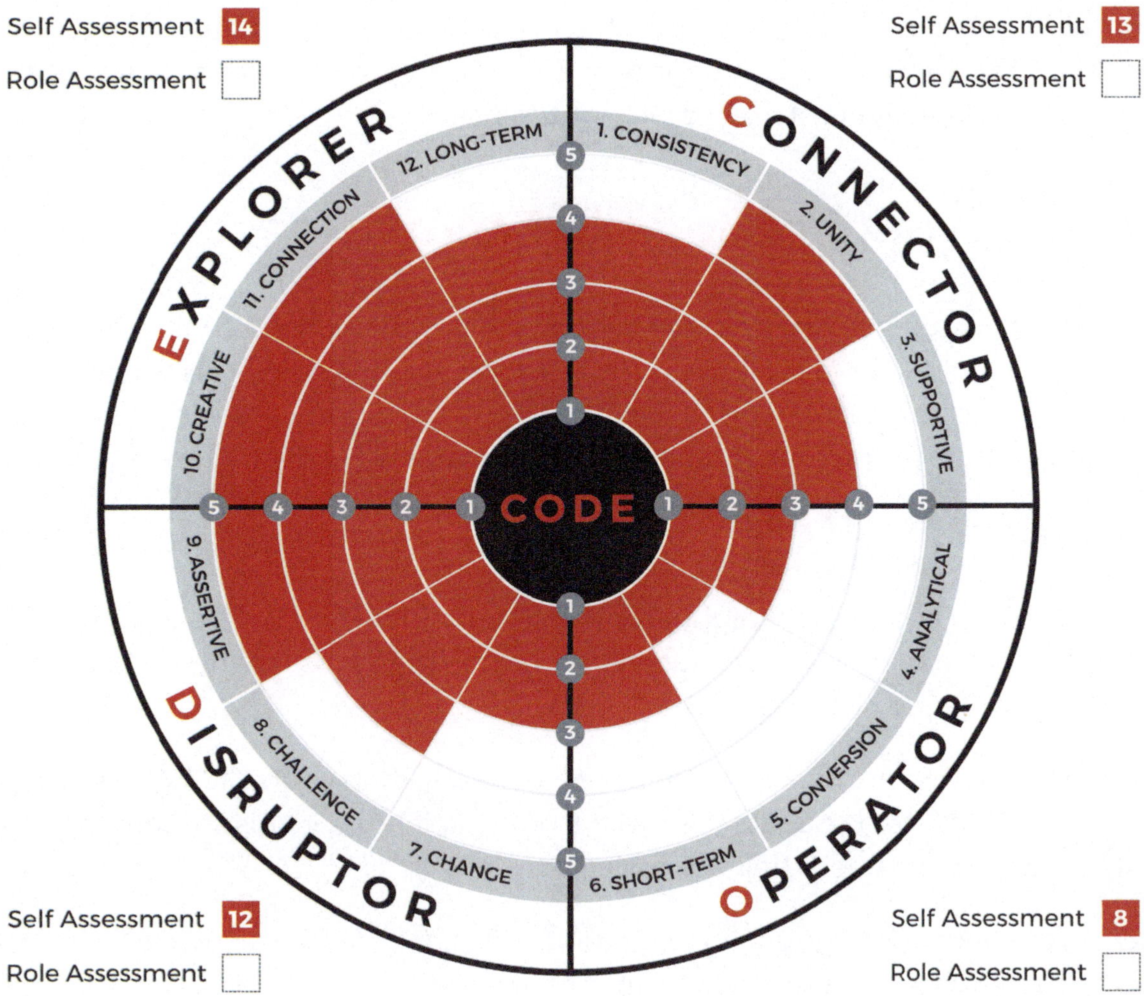

This marketing leader was very effective in the Leadership Team and scored high on many ANCHOR Factors, but were held back by the weaker scores on the ANCHOR Factors associate with Operator.

Understanding the Operator gap gave the opportunity to rebalance their profile by reviewing the shape and skill set of their senior marketing team. In this case they brought in a new senior digital director to complement their skills.

Enhancing your Leadership Team impact

This section looks at self-assessment results combined with the results of a role assessment carried out by a key stakeholder. Again start by asking yourself some questions:

- What is the total scoring for the stakeholder and yourself? Are they scoring you overall higher or lower? Is this simply over or underscoring or is there something more significant?
- What ANCHOR Factors score higher for the stakeholder than yourself? Why are they valuing this more than you rate yourself? Does this matter, is this ANCHOR Factor covered by someone else in the team?
- What ANCHOR Factors are lower for the stakeholder than yourself? Why are they valuing this lower than you rate yourself? Does this matter, is this something you highly value and will need their appreciation?
- What is your lead CODE genre and how does this compare to the CODE the stakeholder gives? How similar or different are you?

In the following example there is good alignment in the ANCHOR Factors at the top of the map between the marketing leader and CEO but you will see some ANCHOR Factors are being rated significantly differently. This is feeding into the CODE – the CEO who carried out the stakeholder assessment has prioritised Operator as the lead genre – O-C-E-D, whilst the marketer has rated themselves Connector led – C-E-O-D. This difference between the CEO and marketer on Operator is important to understand.

Self-assessment:

Self Assessment **10**
Role Assessment

Self Assessment **12**
Role Assessment

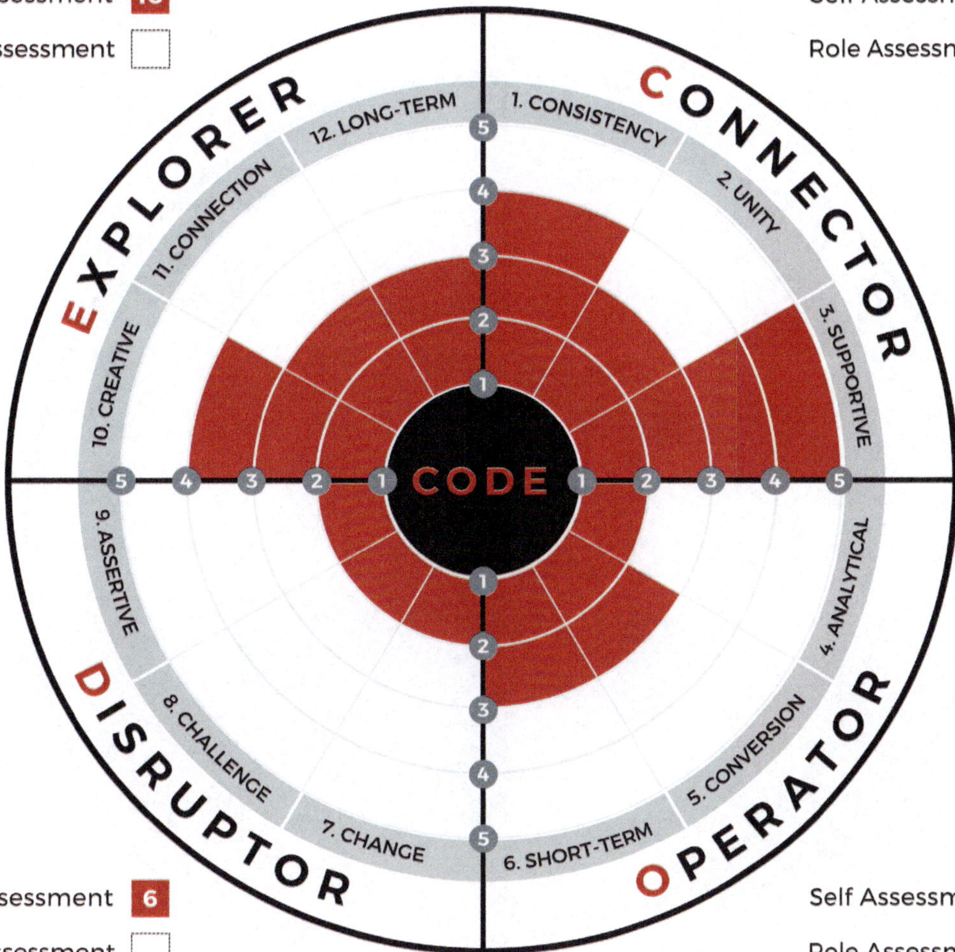

Self Assessment **6**
Role Assessment

Self Assessment **8**
Role Assessment

CEO assessment:

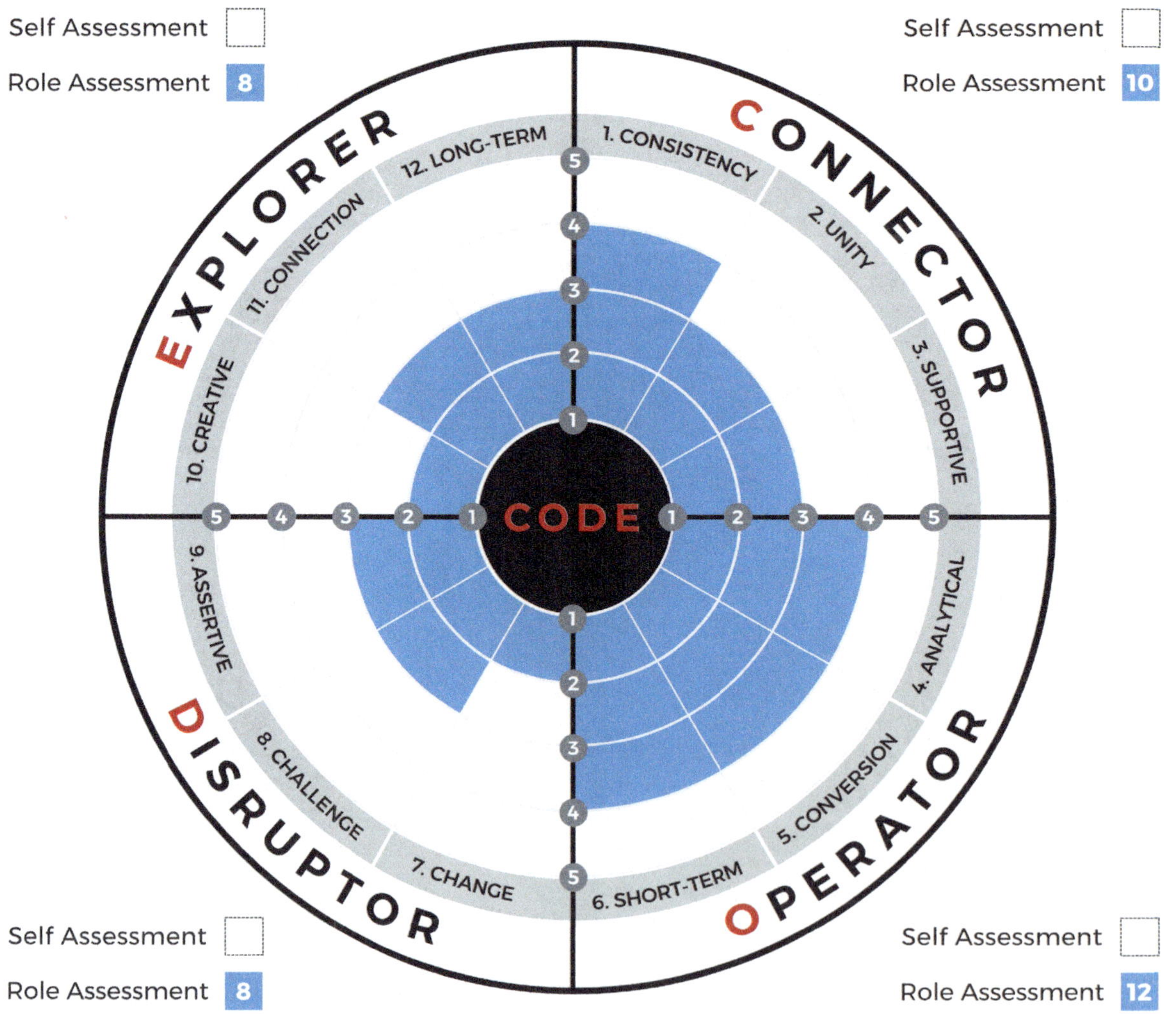

Self and CEO assessment overlay:

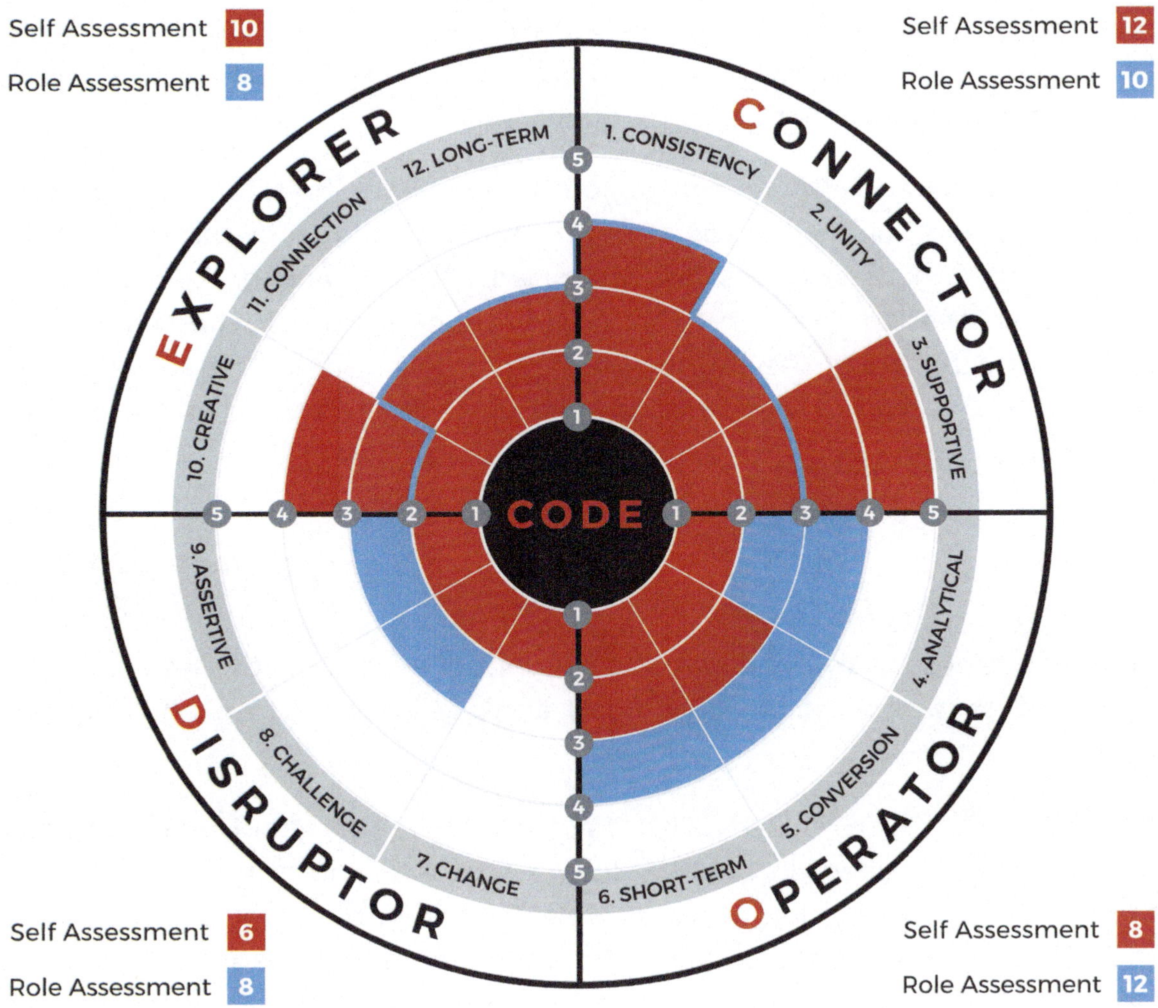

The CEO is scoring higher on the ANCHOR Factors of Assertive, Challenge, Analytical, Conversion and Short-term and lower on Supportive and Creative. The marketer in the CEO's eyes needed to be more of an Operator and make bolder organisational moves with the team. This gap on Operator means the CEO is putting more value on external ANCHOR Factors (Headspace-Output-Results) or, in other words, wanting the marketer to deliver better marketing, as opposed to being involved with internal ANCHOR Factors (Ambition-Network-Capability) and steering the wider business. Only by addressing this area can the marketer enhance their Leadership Team impact more.

In this case the marketer had been central to developing the brand and building a close-knit team, but competitors had made strong progress in digital channels. The CEO had the perception that marketing was not organised correctly and needed to evolve. The marketing leader needed to review the organisational structure and Operator team capabilities with the CEO. Reassuring him the team had these capabilities, or demonstrating the marketing leader had the muscle to review the organisation and make some bold people decisions.

Onboarding or recruiting a new marketing leader

Joining a new business is always a risk. Job descriptions from headhunters aren't always accurate or apply to the immediate job in hand, and psychometric tests and interviews can be superficial.

Information from the CODE and ANCHOR Factors can help. Not only can this assess the marketer but also the role, giving both sides an accurate read of what is really needed. Is the company really looking for a Chief Growth Officer with an Operator bias, or a Chief Marketing Officer with a Connector bias? Applicants can simply take the assessment and a key internal stakeholder can assess the role. How these subsequently marry up can open up a discussion around the CODE and different ANCHOR Factors, giving both sides an opportunity to assess the fit and ask more pertinent questions in the interview about the role's requirements.

Assuming the new marketer has been appointed, the faster they learn the ropes and find their sea legs the better. Onboarding a marketer into a business can be quite a passive high-level talk about strategy or plans, and not about homeostasis, leadership relationships, challenge culture, decision making or street-fighters. This is the stuff a new person really wants and needs to know about and can open up a richer debate:

- Why are some ANCHOR Factor scores for the role high and some low? Is this about capability elsewhere in the team or in the business, or does it say something around the role's responsibilities?
- What is the lead CODE of the role and why? Is this the CODE of a previous marketing leader or like this for a reason?
- Are there long ranging plans the marketer needs to know now? Is there business history which makes the CEO or leadership team nervous in some areas?
- Are there immediate fires in some ANCHOR Factor areas which need to be put out now? Where are storms likely to emerge in the future and what are the resources at hand?
- What is the CEO's agenda? What are the areas they want the marketing leader to focus upon?

In this next example a new marketer was being brought into a new role. A strong digital marketer already existed and could cover the Operator area. They needed a marketing leader who could manage the digital expert and could steer brand development. They needed someone who was stronger on Explorer, more like a Chief Brand Officer but with the ability to strongly manage the team.

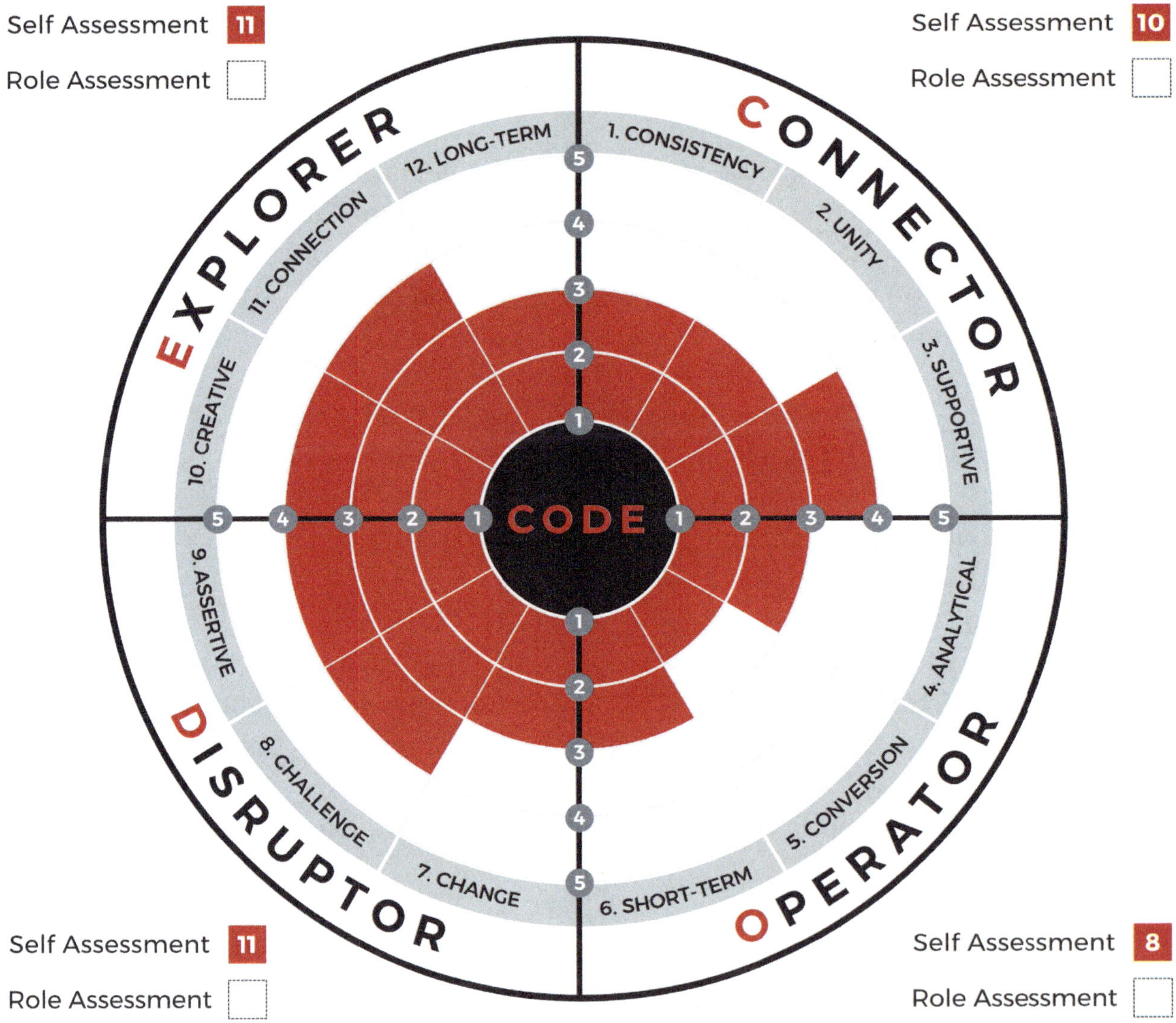
Self Assessment 11
Role Assessment
Self Assessment 10
Role Assessment
EXPLORER
CONNECTOR
OPERATOR
DISRUPTOR
1. CONSISTENCY
2. UNITY
3. SUPPORTIVE
4. ANALYTICAL
5. CONVERSION
6. SHORT-TERM
7. CHANGE
8. CHALLENGE
9. ASSERTIVE
10. CREATIVE
11. CONNECTION
12. LONG-TERM
CODE
1 2 3 4 5
Self Assessment 11
Role Assessment
Self Assessment 8
Role Assessment

The marketer joining had a bias to Disruptor and Explorer, which complimented the digital marketer already in the team. They were strongly customer-centric, could develop the brand and had proven capability in managing a diverse team of marketers across both analogue and digital media.

Becoming a future marketing leader

If you have aspirations to be a future marketing leader, then *The Marketing Leader's CODE* will help you understand the true breadth of the job and map yourself against it. You will have areas which are stronger or weaker and you can think strategically about the moves you make so you gather the broader skills needed.

I made a series of zigzag career moves to build my expertise. From starting my career at Unilever, I moved to Innocent Drinks, then to Mars and on to MoneySuperMarket. Unilever built foundational skills in brand, strategy and insight. Innocent fuelled my passion to be more entrepreneurial and agile. Mars was a highly matrixed organisation where collaboration and alignment were key. MoneySuperMarket was a pure play digital business, which expanded my digital marketing skills. This built my Explorer, Disruptor, Connector and Operator genres.

Some of these moves were horizontal: a different role in a different company but comparable pay. This might not seem logical to everyone, but these moves can be important in the long run. The right horizontal move can accelerate your career and earnings later. I call them zigzag career moves and this enables you to be a rounder marketing leader in the future.

The diagram below oversimplifies the moves, but each new company allowed me to push into new areas and gain new experiences which expanded my marketing leader's CODE and meant that I could take on broader and more challenging future roles. My personality means my strongest bias is more towards Explorer and Connector, but I have the experience to be an Operator or Disruptor as well or ideally work with a strong number 2 with these traits.

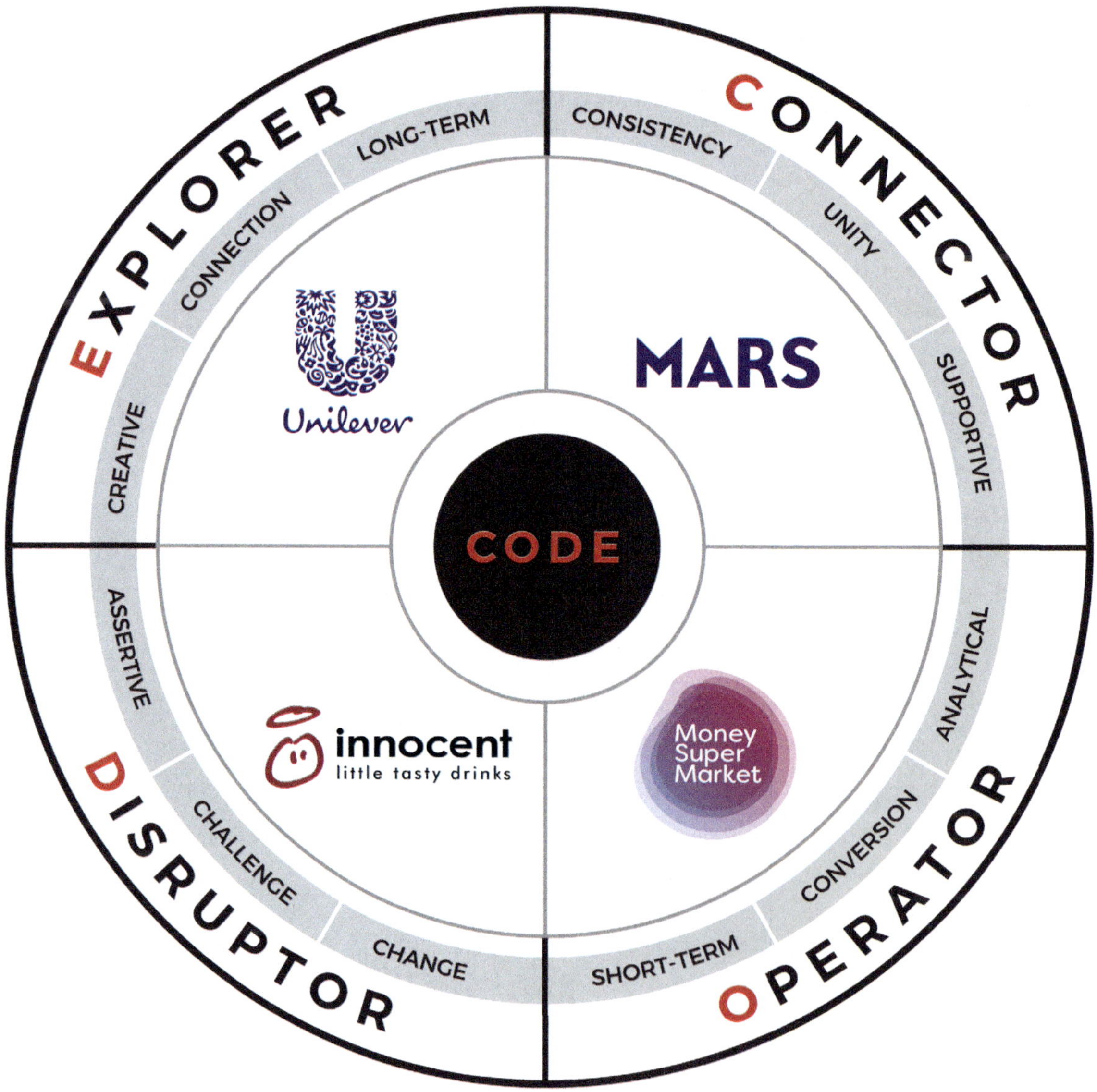

Developing these wider skills doesn't always need to mean changing companies. In my last client side role one of the team asked if they could do an apprenticeship on data literacy, so she could become a fully qualified data technician. It required a pretty hefty amount of work on her part, and some time off, but the courses cost the business nothing and was her pivoting across into the Operator genre. Similarly there are so many course on LinkedIn and others sites that are easy to access and show a personal commitment to self development. Anyone who had made zigzag career moves across the different ANCHOR Factors like this I would look at more favourably than someone who had not.

TACTICS TO TRY

The Marketing Leader's CODE will help you understand yourself and the true breadth of the marketing leadership role.

Being the marketing leader is the best job in the world, but it can be one of the toughest and loneliest. The role has become so diverse, it provides the marketer with enormous opportunities, but with diversity comes misunderstanding across the Leadership Team too. Misunderstanding generally will fall into one of the ANCHOR Factors and unmanaged can become a wider issue. We all know the tense feeling when something just is not landing right and it is so important not to ignore it. This is a tell-tale sign to respond to and the following pages are a series of tactics you might want to try.

The tactics are split into each ANCHOR Factor and grouped together under the different CODE genres. The tactics are designed to help an existing marketing leader show increased presence and influence in an area. They are not designed to replace the core skills and capability to do each ANCHOR Factor, but rather springboards to build upon your current knowledge and expand your impact.

More information on each tool is available at sideminds.com. For further bespoke support in developing capability in any ANCHOR Factor there is also an independent team of specialists at sideminds. Contact support@sideminds.com for more information.

Connector Tactics

Consistency

Having good business practices will help the teams stay focused, motivated and successful. Being empowered with a customer outcome, knowing the guard rails to operate within and how decisions will be made, helps progress to be made faster and more effectively.

1. Ensure a short manageable list of cross company projects are agreed, prioritised and monitored regularly across the Leadership Team. Challenge activity that is not on the list.
2. Create a regular cadence of meetings between the Leadership Team and key project team leaders. Empower the project team and ensure they know the expectations at each check-in point.
3. Set up a clear decision-making framework (RAPID, RACI, DAI etc). Ensure everyone

involved in a project knows their role, who they need to involve and the ultimate decision point.

4. Define and monitor KPIs and/or OKRs consistently across the company. Get resources (money and importantly people) reprioritised and reallocated at each review session.
5. Review the company governance and guard rail principles. Are the company systems roundabouts or traffic lights? Can teams operate independently and effectively within them?
6. Formalise the innovation development and testing process. Lock key parts of the innovation plan into the annual budget setting process, so it becomes more accountable.
7. Review the innovation process and innovation velocity between each stage; expose any internal barriers which are slowing the process down.
8. Review go-to-market effectiveness. Check the executional quality and ensure the teams are empowered to make go/no-go decisions. Can they stop activity or get assistance quickly?

Supportive

How do you adapt your style to get the best out of everyone? How can you help your team and agencies reach their full potential? Some of your team may be the right people in the wrong job. How can you help them succeed and grow?

1. Experiment with a more varied and flexible situational leadership approach that blends prescriptive direction with coaching support.[1]
2. Introduce career ladders, mapping all the roles across marketing and encouraging zigzag career moves internally.
3. Set targets for Diversity, Equality and Inclusion and make sure DEI is discussed in the boardroom. Ensure everyone feels included. Agree Teamship[2] rules and understand what gets the best out of each other.

4. Carry out a 9-box assessment of the team and develop an action plan. Give key high performers projects or opportunities to grow and develop skills. Do not be ageist, accelerate promotion of talent and find the blend of youth and experience.
5. Get the external agencies/partners to have more accountability linked to performance; create fair and motivating remuneration models and independently review.
6. Carry out 360-degree feedback; be a role model giving and receiving real-time feedback; show you listen and adapt as this builds trust and effectiveness.[3]
7. Get behind the surface script you see day-to-day. Care about how people are really doing. Ask them about their energy levels? How is their personal, career, financial, physical and home/community well-being?
8. Remove historical cognitive bias in performance reviews by not letting people see historical rating before giving a manager review. Be aware of your own bias impact in meetings.

Unity

The Leadership Team needs healthy debate and then alignment on an agreed set of actions that are clearly communicated to the business. Look at how well you are working together as a Leadership Team and how well you are giving the same message and direction.

1. Write a charter on how decisions are made in the Leadership Team. Disagree, discuss, deploy. Make sure enough discussion happens and then everyone commits.
2. Lead the development of the business vision and overall strategy with the Leadership Team. Involve high potential employees in defining the company purpose, mission and values.
3. Bring together top-down targets with bottom-up diagnostics and evaluation. Start to focus on agreed shared customer outcomes across the Leadership and wider teams.
4. Align objectives across the Leadership Team and define interdependencies between

departments. Review these shared priorities at least quarterly with cross functional teams.

5. Define the Leadership Team's collective role, purpose and ways of working. Create a pre-aread culture or follow the Amazon way[4] and set time aside in the meeting to read the pre-read.
6. Carry out a Leadership Team exercise, so you know each other better and build trust; more trust means more effectiveness[5]; make the Leadership Team a safe place to challenge.
7. Introduce a critical review process to assess past Leadership Team behaviours and activity. Reflect on what is working and what isn't and apply learnings.
8. Differentiate key projects from business-as-usual across all departments and have an ongoing check-in with teams to ensure progress is being made.

Operator Tactics

Analytical

The business relies upon facts and insights being presented in a coherent way so that decisions can be made. Think about the information you have now and how fit for purpose it is. How can decision-making be enhanced? How can you stay abreast of wider technical advances?

1. Define and monitor leading and lagging indicators. Keep focused on the 'now' but ensure future issues are discussed and acted upon early.
2. Ensure analysis has been done to ensure fact-based Leadership Team discussions. Always give a clear sight of the prize and with limited data, make logical assumptions

and show how you have challenged your own thinking.

3. Review the timeliness of data based decision-making. Are the Leadership Team an accelerator or bottle neck which keeps requiring more analysis? Review the need for certainty vs bravery with the Leadership Team.
4. Review the marketing attribution system. It is hard to get a perfect solution but ensure it is appropriate and consistently used across the business (geographical regions, business teams).
5. Introduce a fast test and learn process to rapidly validate hypotheses in 1–2 weeks and prototype ideas quickly.[6] Be able to scale ideas that work at pace. Get buy-in from the Leadership Team to this approach.
6. Review your approach to data management and check you have the right customer and/or data management plan. Find ways to ensure the data is clean, unduplicated, updated and enriched.
7. Lead the development of an AI and Martech roadmap. Spend time with the CTO and CPO, understanding technology opportunities.
8. Drive the use of new tools and methodologies in the data team. Create partnerships with non-competitive businesses on insight methodology and insight. Pinpoint key companies to follow.
9. Create a single KPI tracking dashboard and marketing scorecard that covers all marketing channels.

Conversion

When the customer is on a buying mission your brand needs to be available, relevant and buyable. The customer's needs at each stage have to be understood and the experience optimised to make the buying journey effective.

1. Make it easier to buy; review the customer pain points and decision trees. Go step by step through the journey and check you have the essential hygiene factors correct to

make your product/service buyable.

2. Assess if you have the right message at the right time. Review how strong these messages are compared to competitive brands.
3. Think about the killer data facts and propositions you would like to have to drive conversion. Think about how you could get the data to support these propositions. Be imaginative. It can be done!
4. Set a clear role and KPI for each marketing activity down the purchase funnel. Ensure upper funnel activity is measured differently to lower funnel and the Leadership Team buy in to these measures.
5. Carry out a communication audit. Remove outdated or poor content; review site mapping; check LRDs/backlinks; check paid media is not underperforming due to negative trolling.
6. Find ways to be contextually relevant with your campaigns. From tactically leveraging current events, to using geographic extensions, and targeting by life stage.
7. Manage and optimise brand owned and third-party sites. Check the landing pages are correct for customers coming to the site.
8. Review the balance of brand spend to generic spend and sales promotion. Play the devil's advocate with the Leadership Team on managing the balance of short-term and long-term.

Short Term

Marketers need to be get stuck into daily sales and be scrappers who fight to hit targets. Finding opportunities to optimise sales and keep the business focused on delivering the goals for the month, quarter or year. How do you encourage this behaviour and ensure the annual plan is delivered without compromising the future?

1. Walk the talk on performance; get out on the street, in-store or online and see what is going on. Action speaks louder than words.

2. Set up a 'Fast Action Squad' to define opportunities that can be accelerated quickly. Let this team define the resources they need to get new activity to market quickly.
3. Carry out root cause analysis to define the issues and stack rank solutions. Make assumptions based upon logic and test theories quickly.
4. For retail sales businesses, review the rate of sale per distribution point and optimise the range. Check you have a competitive marketing mix (5Ps) for the segment you are operating in.
5. Look at the opportunity for gap filling with innovation that has a low impact on resources, for example, new distribution channels, special editions or new price fighter ranges.
6. Have pre-agreed sales promotion tactics to deploy at short notice. Pre-test the activity and understand competitive response.
7. Review media channels, focus on highest value returns or proximity to purchase. Keep an open brief for last minute media opportunities (distress sales).
8. Look at first party customer data sets and performance tracking; are there opportunities to change creative, improve re-contact chase cycles, re-target rested audiences or introduce new cross sales?

Disruptor Tactics

Change

Driving change is not easy and for credibility the marketing leader needs to understand the existing practices first. You need to understand the current approach then find like-minded peers who share your views and look at opportunities to test your thinking.

1. Find a small project to tackle in a different way or with a different supplier. Get a small win you can then leverage on a bigger issue. This is an ideal step if moving to agile working practices.
2. Write a corporate change story with the CEO. Why is this approach better for the company, the employees, the customers etc? Get the Leadership Team to write

personal change stories for their team.

3. Be uninhibited and get the team to think like entrepreneurs or a start-up. How would they break a project down into small manageable steps or affordable chunks?
4. Encourage more purposeful innovation with divergent and convergent thinking. Frame innovation more precisely and introduce a process to stretch and then channel thinking.
5. Look at alternative business models and bring in external best practice. Follow innovative businesses in key market adjacencies and keep the Leadership Team informed.
6. Set up real-time customer sentiment trackers (NPS, social media, perception monitoring) and a rolling programme to uncover customer insights. Keep the Leadership Team connected to the customer.
7. Define the close in innovation adjacencies and develop an M&A blueprint, with key target companies to monitor. Check innovation project owners are not also doing wider operational roles, which are taking priority.
8. Introduce an intelligence strategy to ensure all customer information is effectively shared across the company.

Challenge

Understand the group dynamics at play in the boardroom. Where are the informal alliances and who are the real decision makers? Work out the areas you feel passionate about and want to challenge the approach.

1. Review the Leadership Team interactions and decision-making. Discuss how bias may be influencing decisions in the boardroom and test techniques to manage the effects. Develop a toolkit to counter cognitive bias in decision-making.
2. Define the key issues that hold the business back; get them validated, understood and kept front of mind. Ensure these issues are not misrepresented or ignored by the

Leadership Team.

3. Bring environmental, ethical or social challenges to the boardroom. Do not let changes be kicked down the road, have an environmental pledge and don't greenwash.
4. Promote customer-centric thinking and behaviours from the boardroom downwards. Bring competitive intelligence to the boardroom; discuss activity and scenario plan.
5. Show your killer instinct and stop non-prioritised activity (stack rank risk vs return). Be ruthless and focus resource on what really matters.
6. Encourage an 'obligation to dissent' culture; be the devil's advocate and ask the questions about what might go wrong. Make it a Leadership Team value to participate in debates.
7. Scrutinise cross company business cases to ensure targets and delivery dates are realistic.
8. Introduce monthly 30-minute power time exercises on challenging topics: 10 minutes of silent written download, 10 minutes of silent connection building and 10 minutes of discussion.

Assertive

Your team is your most important asset. You need to create an environment where talent can thrive, which can mean making some bold decisions around structure and people. Give your high potentials bandwidth to grow and be assertive on low potentials.

1. Turn the business strategy into a marketing strategy with clear customer goals for the team to own.
2. Give the team a clear sense of purpose and identity, with individual responsibility and ownership.
3. Encourage trust, mutual respect and accountability and be clear and consistent on action standards. Make time to get to know the team – trust takes time to be built and

investment pays off in the long run.

4. Keep the organisational structure linked to strategy. Be prepared to reorganise and reset team priorities, so short-term business priorities are addressed.
5. Get company performance metrics cascaded from the business and marketing strategy to the individual. Deconstruct your own personal KPIs.
6. Encourage continuous learning and reflection; help individuals define their North Star, personal SWOT and development plan.
7. Measure and celebrate team and individual success. Develop a reward, retention and career mentoring programme for the high achievers.
8. Audit the team and identify critical skill gaps; bring in critical talent but at a higher performance level[7] or develop team from within.

Explorer Tactics

Creative

Creative, step-change ideas can come from anywhere. It is important to establish an environment where everyone recognises ideas will be valued and hunches are allowed to germinate.

1. Turn a business challenge into customer to/from analysis – what needs to change and be different?
2. Use creative techniques to address business issues e.g. Edward de Bono's 6 Thinking Hats.[8]
3. Carry out 'what if' analysis and explore new potential outcomes. Carry out small tests

to validate.[9]

4. Get closer to customers by understanding prioritised audiences at a category, shopper and customer level.
5. Look for big emotionally charged ideas that generate a reaction (entertain, shock, inspire). Look for higher order benefit using a benefit ladder; lift rational features into emotional benefits.
6. Encourage the team to enter awards and get recognition from their peers. Reward creativity and smart thinking.
7. Drive the ongoing development of 'new news' to keep the brand front of mind.
8. Create a marketing calendar of compelling events that bring the customer back.

Connection

Customers can have relationships with brands that last a lifetime. These brands have created a connection which means it transcends all others. How strong is your brand and how are you cultivating a relationship through different media channels?

1. Define the brand positioning and value propositions; be clear why the brand exists and is better than others.
2. Create a brand manifesto, with a purpose and mission that acts as a beacon for communications.[10]
3. Align the business behind a consistent visual identity, tone of voice, archetype and distinctive assets.[11] [12]
4. Create a ubiquitous omni-channel experience that is relevant to the customer's lifecycle with the brand. Make the brand memorable and distinctive for the widest audience.
5. Understand what customers are interested in (social listening) and create a conversation calendar.
6. Understand the drivers of consideration and trial; what are the generic drivers and

what are differentiators?

7. Build brand trust, by developing a plan to address customer tensions and change perceptions.
8. Increase customer online registration through an effective value exchange. Understand what is in it for the customer, so if they sign up they get genuine added value in return.

Long Term

Marketing is not just about converting customers today but about finding long term revenue streams and guiding the business towards these goals. This puts marketing at the heart of business strategy.

1. Lead the strategy process, gather key Leadership Team's concerns and introduce a rapid-testing or insight process to help narrow choices.
2. Carry out segmentation studies to define the key opportunity areas.
3. Define the priority markets and channels using a variety of lenses (GMAC, Growth, Competitive advantage).
4. Define the rules of the game to win in a category; understand the 5Ps and what is needed to be truly competitive.
5. Run investment scenarios on various strategies; look at the long/short-term investment balance. Carry out econometric analysis and use to help define budget setting.
6. Carry out gap filling innovation analysis and define areas to build, expand and disrupt.
7. Develop a clarion call or storytelling narrative to motivate the internal team; adapt the clarion call to motivate and inspire long-term investors.
8. Carry out competitive war gaming to define competitor moves; deconstruct competitive activity. Review Share of Voice to Share of Market; product/packaging 60/40 testing. Simulate events and scenario plan.

Notes

1. O'Neill, M. (2011). *Executive Coaching with Backbone and Heart.* Jossey-Bass.
2. Woodward, C. (2005). *Winning!: The Path to Rugby World Cup Glory.* Hodder.
3. Zenger Folkman. (November, 2020). 6 Top Behaviours That Cause A Loss Of Trust. Zenger Folkman. https://zengerfolkman.com/articles/6-top-behaviors-that-cause-a-loss-of-trust/
4. Locke, T. (October, 2019). 'Jeff Bezos: This is the "smartest thing we ever did" at Amazon'. CNBC. https://www.cnbc.com/2019/10/14/jeff-bezos-this-is-the-smartest-thing-we-ever-did-at-amazon.html
5. Covey, S., and Merrill, R. (2008). *The Speed of Trust: The One Thing That Changes Everything*. Simon & Schuster.
6. Bland, J., Osterwalder, A. (2020). *Testing Business Ideas.* Wiley.
7. Amazon Staff. (2019). What is an Amazon bar raiser? About Amazon. https://www.aboutamazon.com/news/workplace/amazon-bar-raiser
8. The de Bono Group. *Six Thinking Hats.* De Bono Group. https://www.debonogroup.com/services/core-programs/six-thinking-hats/
9. Bland, J., Osterwalder, A. (2020). *Testing Business Ideas.* Wiley.
10. Morgan, A. (1999). *Eating the Big Fish. How Challenger Brands can compete against Brand Leaders*. Adweek Media.
11. Mark, M. and Pearson, C. (2001). *The Hero and the Outlaw: Building Extraordinary Brands Through the Power of Archetypes.* McGraw-Hill Education.
12. Sharp, B. (2010). *How Brands Grow: What Marketers Don't Know.* Oxford University Press.

NEXT STEPS AND FURTHER SUPPORT

'Life isn't about waiting for the storm to pass ... it's learning to dance in the rain.'
Unknown

Being the marketing leader is the best job in the world, but it can be one of the toughest and loneliest. The role has become so diverse, it provides the marketer enormous opportunities, but with diversity comes misunderstanding across the Leadership Team too. I can not think of any other leadership job where there has been over 50% increase in new skill capabilities in a 10 year period.[1] The marketer can be managing multiple storms across the business, which unless managed carefully can drag the marketer down, slow progress and sometimes leading to the marketer's early exit. Sadly we know from Spencer Stuart[2] the median tenure for top marketing leaders is now just over 2 years, the lowest of the entire Leadership Team.

It really doesn't need to be like this. Every marketing leadership role and every marketer is different, but there are core skills and capabilities that are universal for success in the role. *The Marketing Leader's CODE* explains what these are through the CODE and ANCHOR Factor tools. These help to break down the skills and capabilities of every role and every marketer, so the right person can fit the right role and development gaps or misunderstanding can be minimised. By doing this the marketing leader can be more effective and more successful over the long term. I certainly wish I knew then what I know now. It would have helped me navigate the tough times better and have even more good times.

Business is, however, tough and there are endless storms which will hit the boat. So whilst *The Marketing Leader's CODE* gives a skills framework to help you prepare, the wind and the rain will still hit the boat and the marketing leader should think about their personal resilience and well-being plan. Part of this is understanding your social networks. I relied upon my family and marketing peers, who listened, helped me think and ensured my well-being didn't deteriorate. A risk we can all face and explained by Heidi Godman in her article in Harvard Health Publishing.[3]

Networks like this can take time to develop, which isn't always possible in a busy marketing role. If you lack a network or want more ongoing support and guidance, sideminds.com can help. Set up by marketing leaders for marketing leaders, it uses the principles from *The Marketing Leader's CODE* to help the marketer navigate the role and relationships better, so they feel more confident and make an impact. To find out more go to sideminds.com or email support@sideminds.com.

Notes

1. PHD Contributors. (2022). *Shift. A Marketing Rethink.* PHD Marketing.
2. Welch, G., and Sanderson, R. (April, 2022). CMO Tenure Study: Women outnumber men for first time in CMO role. Spencer Stuart. https://www.spencerstuart.com/research-and-insight/cmo-tenure-study-women-outnumber-men-for-first-time-in-cmo-role
3. Godman, H. (November, 2021). Can Friends Who Listen Help Protect Your Memory And Thinking Skills? Harvard Health Publishing. www.health.harvard.edu/mind-and-mood/can-friends-who-listen-help-protect-your-memory-and-thinking-skills

ABOUT THE AUTHOR

Gareth Helm has over 30 years' experience in marketing businesses all around the world, with half of this time working in the Leadership Team. Starting out as a graduate trainee with Unilever in the Middle East he went on to be the marketing leader or adviser on a wide variety of brands in different stages of their life cycle. From new start-ups, to some of the world's largest and favourite brands:

McDonald's	Mars	HomeServe	Checkatrade
MoneySuperMarket	Zoopla	uSwitch	PrimeLocation
Money	Innocent Drinks	Tails (N)	Higgidy (N)
Bear Snacks (A)	allplants (A)	Purple Bricks (N)	

Gareth was recognised as one of the top 100 most effective marketers in 2021 by Marketing Week, is a Fellow at The Marketing Academy and trained in Executive Coaching by Ashridge Hult International Business School.

In 2022 he set up sideminds.com, a marketing leadership service for marketing leaders.

Midway through Gareth's marketing career he found out he was dyslexic. He realised it had helped him think differently to others and create models to get around the day-to-day processing issues dyslexics can experience. *The Marketing Leader's CODE* is one of the models.

A: Adviser, N: Non-Executive Director

REFERENCES

Amazon Staff. (2019). *What is an Amazon bar raiser?* About Amazon. https://www.aboutamazon.com/news/workplace/amazon-bar-raiser

Argyris, C. (1991). *Teaching smart people how to learn.* Harvard Business Review. https://hbr.org/1991/05/teaching-smart-people-how-to-learn/

Barta, T., and Barwise, P. (2017). *The 12 Powers of a Marketing Leader.* McGraw-Hill Education.

Binet, L., and Field, P. (2013). *The Long and the Short of It: Balancing Short and Long-Term Marketing Strategies.* Institute of Practitioners in Advertising.

Bland, J., Osterwalder, A. (2020). *Testing Business Ideas.* Wiley.

Carayol, R. (2017). *Spike. What are you great at?* LID Publishing.

Collins, J., and Porras, J. (1995). *Built To Last: Successful Habits of Visionary Companies.* Random House Business.

Covey, S., and Merrill, R. (2008). *The Speed of Trust: The One Thing That Changes Everything.* Simon & Schuster.

Cowling, H. (July, 2022). *The Business Case for Web3.* The CMO Club Innovation Forum. https://thecmoclub.com/

de Haaff, B. (2017). *Loveability. How to build a business that people love and be happy doing it.* Greenleaf Book Group.

Edmondson, A. (May, 2019). Harvard Business Review. https://hbr.org/2019/05/boeing-and-the-importance-of-encouraging-employees-to-speak-up/

Field, P. (2015). *Creativity and Effectiveness with Peter Field.* Thinkbox. www.thinkbox.tv/creative/insight/creativity-and-effectiveness-with-peter-field/

Folkman, J. (2019). *Extraordinary Leader 360-Degree Survey.* ZengerFolkman.com https://zengerfolkman.com/wp-content/uploads/2019/08/EL360Survey_WP-2019.pdf

Ford, H. (unknown). www.thehenryford.org

Forrester team. (October, 2021). *Predictions 2022: CMOs Emerge as Emboldened Business Leaders*. Forrester. www.forrester.com/blogs/predictions-2022-b2c-cmo-trends/

Gadiesh, O., and MacArthur, H. (2009). *Lessons from Private Equity Any Company Can Use.* Harvard Business Press.

Germain, D. (2009). *A Book About Innocent: Our Story and Some Things We've Learned.* Michael Joseph.

Godman, H. (November, 2021). *Can Friends Who Listen Help Protect Your Memory And Thinking Skills?* Harvard Health Publishing. www.health.harvard.edu/mind-and-mood/can-friends-who-listen-help-protect-your-memory-and-thinking-skills

Greenwood, W., and Fennell, B. (2021). *World Class: How to Lead, Learn and Grow like Champion.* Penguin.

Grove, A. (1985). *High Output Management.* Random House USA Inc; 1st Vintage Books ed edition.

Jennings, J., and Haughton,L. (2007). *It's Not the Big that Eat the Small ... It's the Fast that Eat the Slow*. Harper Collins.

Kahneman, D., Sibony, O. and Sunstein, C. (2022). *Noise: A Flaw in Human Judgement.* Publisher. William Collins.

Kahneman, D. (2012). *Thinking, Fast and Slow.* Penguin.

Kite, G. (unknown). *The Wrong and The Real of It. Magic Numbers.* www.magicnumbers.co.uk/articles/the-wrong-and-the-real-of-it/

Lencioni, P. (2002). *The Five Dysfunctions of a team.* Jossey-Bass.

Lewis, M. (2003). *Moneyball: The Art of Winning an Unfair Game.* W.W. Norton and Company.

Locke, T. (October, 2019). Jeff Bezos: *This is the 'smartest thing we ever did' at Amazon.* CNBC. https://www.cnbc.com/2019/10/14/jeff-bezos-this-is-the-smartest-thing-we-ever-did-at-amazon.html

Mankins, M., and Steele, R. (July- August, 2005). *Turning Great Strategy into Great Performance.* Harvard Business Review. https://hbr.org/2005/07/turning-great-strategy-into-great-performance

Market Leader. (Spring 2006). *Empower. The Marketing Society.* http://www.marketingsociety.com/the-library/marketing-directors-first-100-days/

Mark, M. and Pearson, C. (2001). *The Hero and the Outlaw: Building Extraordinary Brands Through the Power of Archetypes.* McGraw-Hill Education.

Marquet, D. (2015). *Turn the Ship Around!: A True Story of Building Leaders by Breaking the Rules.* Penguin.

Morgan, A. (1999). *Eating the Big Fish. How Challenger Brands can compete against Brand Leaders.* Adweek Media.

O'Neill, M. (2011). *Executive Coaching with Backbone and Heart.* Jossey-Bass.

PHD Contributors. (2022). *Shift. A Marketing Rethink.* PHD Marketing.

Phillip Jones, J. (January, 1990). *Ad Spending: Growing Market Share.* Harvard Business Review. www.hbr.org/1990/01/ad-spending-growing-market-share

PwC. (2019). *CEO turnover at record high; successors following long serving CEOs struggling according to PwC's Strategy & Global Study.* PwC. https://www.pwc.com/gx/en/news-room/press-releases/2019/ceo-turnover-record-high.html/

Ritson, M. (September, 2020). *'Bothism' is the cure for marketers' fascination with pointless conflict.* Marketing Week. https://www.marketingweek.com/ritson-bothism-cure-marketers-fascination-conflict/

Ritson, M. (2020). *Brand size, creativity main drivers of effectiveness.* WARC. www.warc.com/newsandopinion/news/brand-size-creativity-main-drivers-of-effectiveness/43074

Rossman, J. (2014). *The Amazon Way: 14 Leadership Principles Behind the World's Most Disruptive Company.* Clyde Hill Publishing.

Sharp, B. (2010). *How Brands Grow: What Marketers Don't Know.* Oxford University Press.

The de Bono Group. *Six Thinking Hats.* De Bono Group. https://www.debonogroup.com/services/core-programs/six-thinking-hats/

Welch, G., and Sanderson, R. (April, 2022). *CMO Tenure Study: Women outnumber men for first time in CMO role.* Spencer Stuart. https://www.spencerstuart.com/research-and-insight/cmo-tenure-study-women-outnumber-men-for-first-time-in-cmo-role

Whitler, K., and Morgan, N. (July- August, 2017). *The trouble with CMOs.* Harvard Business Review. https://hbr.org/2017/07/the-trouble-with-cmos

Woodward, C. (2005). *Winning!: The Path to Rugby World Cup Glory.* Hodder.

Zenger Folkman. (November, 2020). *6 Top Behaviours That Cause A Loss Of Trust*. Zenger Folkman. https://zengerfolkman.com/articles/6-top-behaviors-that-cause-a-loss-of-trust/

APPENDIX

In either assessment, read each statement and answer with a score of 1–5.

The scoring guide:

5 = Almost always
4 = Usually
3 = Sometimes
2 = Rarely
1 = Almost never

The scoring guide is the same for both the self-assessment and the stakeholder assessment.

The stakeholder assessment is focused on the role, so make sure the stakeholder doing the review does not think about you personally. There is no right or wrong, just write scores in the white box next to each statement.

	ANCHOR Factors Quick Self-Assessment (Part 1)	Answer (1–5)
Q1	Highly systematic and actively ensures there is clear prioritisation, governance and communication of projects and initiatives within the Leadership Team and across the wider business.	______
Q2	Data based decision maker, who deeply interrogates facts to make commercial decisions and, when relevant, understands the detail and benefits of new technology approaches.	______
Q3	Thrives on change, likes to work with the CEO on a change agenda, short cutting the existing approach and finding new solutions that are better for the business and customer.	______
Q4	Talented creatively, who ensures every customer touchpoint is a high quality experience and makes valuable imaginative leaps, which aren't always obvious to others.	______
Q5	Politically savvy and builds strong alliances across the Leadership Team, helps make progress by getting collective alignment and agreement to key tasks amongst the key leaders.	______
Q6	Optimisation expert focused on acquiring customers as cost effectively as possible, looks carefully at the customer journey and uses marketing techniques like direct response to drive conversion to sale.	______

Almost never	Rarely	Sometimes	Usually	Almost always
1	2	3	4	5

ANCHOR Factors Quick Self-Assessment (Part 2)		Answer (1–5)
Q7	Challenging and forthright, sticks their neck out for what they believe in, brings truths to the Leadership Team which other people ignore, known for driving important debate within the Leadership Team.	______
Q8	Curious about customer needs and creates emotive propositions and multi-layer communication campaigns that make the brand/business highly relevant to the customer.	______
Q9	People-centric situational leader, who skilfully manages intercompany conflicts and makes everyone in the marketing team feel well supported, valued and aligned under a clear strategy.	______
Q10	Delivers the performance results that are needed, closely follows sales reporting and makes rapid tactical decisions to ensure the short-term targets are met daily, weekly or monthly.	______
Q11	Sets a high standard for the team to follow, rewards performance and promotes high performers, makes rapid decisions about under performance and boldly changes the organisational structure to deliver strategy.	______
Q12	Future focused, finds the most valuable future revenue streams and creates a coherent strategy and unifying clarion call for the business to follow.	______

Almost never	Rarely	Sometimes	Usually	Almost always
1	2	3	4	5

	ANCHOR Factors Quick Stakeholder Role Assessment (Part 1)	Answer (1–5)
Q1	Highly systematic and actively ensures there is clear prioritisation, governance and communication of projects and initiatives within the Leadership Team and across the wider business.	________
Q2	Data based decision maker, who deeply interrogates facts to make commercial decisions and, when relevant, understands the detail and benefits of new technology approaches.	________
Q3	Thrives on change, likes to work with the CEO on a change agenda, short cutting the existing approach and finding new solutions that are better for the business and customer.	________
Q4	Talented creatively, who ensures every customer touchpoint is a high quality experience and makes valuable imaginative leaps, which aren't always obvious to others.	________
Q5	Politically savvy and builds strong alliances across the Leadership Team, helps make progress by getting collective alignment and agreement to key tasks amongst the key leaders.	________
Q6	Optimisation expert focused on acquiring customers as cost effectively as possible, looks carefully at the customer journey and uses marketing techniques like direct response to drive conversion to sale.	________

Almost never	Rarely	Sometimes	Usually	Almost always
1	2	3	4	5

	ANCHOR Factors Quick Stakeholder Role Assessment (Part 2)	Answer (1–5)
Q7	Challenging and forthright, sticks their neck out for what they believe in, brings truths to the Leadership Team which other people ignore, known for driving important debate within the Leadership Team.	________
Q8	Curious about customer needs and creates emotive propositions and multi-layer communication campaigns that make the brand/business highly relevant to the customer.	________
Q9	People-centric situational leader, who skilfully manages intercompany conflicts and makes everyone in the marketing team feel well supported, valued and aligned under a clear strategy.	________
Q10	Delivers the performance results that are needed, closely follows sales reporting and makes rapid tactical decisions to ensure the short-term targets are met daily, weekly or monthly.	________
Q11	Sets a high standard for the team to follow, rewards performance and promotes high performers, makes rapid decisions about under performance and boldly changes the organisational structure to deliver strategy.	________
Q12	Future focused, finds the most valuable future revenue streams and creates a coherent strategy and unifying clarion call for the business to follow.	________

Almost never	Rarely	Sometimes	Usually	Almost always
1	2	3	4	5

You can calculate your self-assessment CODE by transferring your score onto the table below, being sure to put the correct answer against each question and then adding the column to give a total out of 15.

Self-Assessment

Connector	Operator	Disruptor	Explorer
Q1______	Q2______	Q3______	Q4______
Q5______	Q6______	Q7______	Q8______
Q9______	Q10_____	Q11_____	Q12_____
Total C_____	Total O_____	Total D_____	Total E_____

Similarly you can calculate the role CODE by transferring the scores your stakeholder has given for each question onto the following table.

Stakeholder Assessment

Connector	Operator	Disruptor	Explorer
Q1______	Q2______	Q3______	Q4______
Q5______	Q6______	Q7______	Q8______
Q9______	Q10_____	Q11_____	Q12_____
Total C_____	Total O_____	Total D_____	Total E_____

The Marketing Leader's CODE

Self Assessment ☐
Role Assessment ☐

Self Assessment ☐
Role Assessment ☐

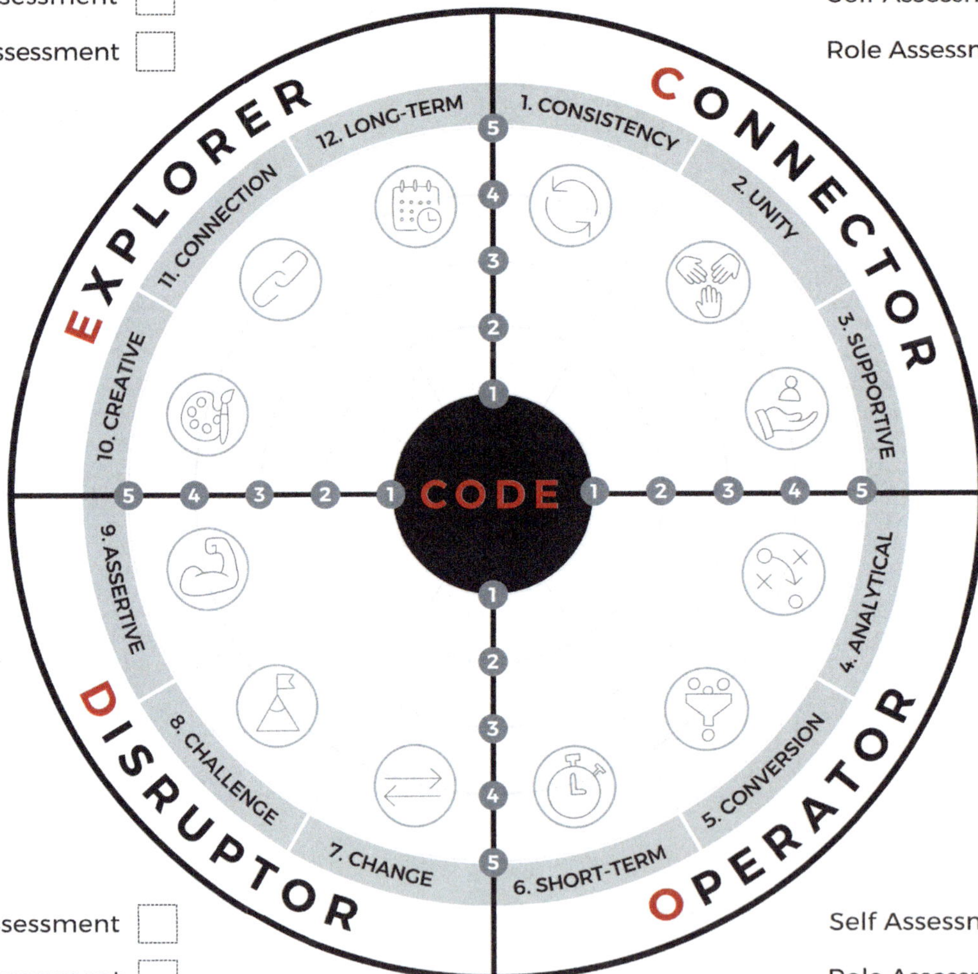

Self Assessment ☐
Role Assessment ☐

Self Assessment ☐
Role Assessment ☐

ACKNOWLEDGEMENTS

Writing a book is never something I intended to do. It came out of a crisis – I had lost my job and was rebuilding my confidence. As I made this journey, I owe enormous gratitude to many people. Some specific people I would like to recognise are:

Piers Fallowfield-Cooper, a dyslexic like me, who was writing a book and introduced me to Debs Jenkins, who guided me through the writing and publishing journey.

Thomas Barta, Richard Harpin, Alex Chesterman OBE, Richard Reed, Frans Leenaars, Dawn Spencer, Gemma Buggins, Alistair Macrow, Pete Markey, Yilmaz Erceyes, Richard Cole, Antoinette Benoit, Colin Whaley, Joanne Savage, Colin Mitchell, Vikaas Saxena, Pip Heywood, Ben Caunter, Jonathon Petrides, Alex Batchelor, Phil Toms, Paul Colback, Lucas Bergmans, Debbie Cooke, David Buch, Vicky Harrop and Jayr Cuario, who all made contributions which helped focus the content.

The Marketing Academy Fellowship 2021, Sherilyn Shackell and Syl Saller CBE for the encouragement to finish the book.

My family, who have been coaches, copywriters, designers and illustrators.

Printed in Great Britain
by Amazon

21352519R00086